What others a ‖‖‖‖‖‖‖‖‖‖ ut this book:

"I bought your book off the internet because I just love fountains. I was thrilled to read it and learn everything I could about making an indoor fountain. I came up with several ideas that I have already begun working on." – Cari Partridge, Grapevine, TX

"I received your book. I can barely put it down. It's the most informative, beautiful book on the subject that I've seen. I've already picked up a few special materials and can't wait to get started. Thank you so much for producing such a wonderful guide. The historical information is just incredible. I've always been one who wants to know the why's of everything and you've certainly provided the answers. I know I'll be ordering more. I enjoy immensely reading Design on Tap, your indoor fountain monthly." – Chantal Chamblee, Los Angeles, CA

"Just to let you know how much I am enjoying the book. It is just a brainstormer for me – all sorts of ideas. I have found so much comfort, peace, and spirit from my fountain." – Mary Haislip, Chattanooga, TN

"We love the book! This fountain building is soooo coooool!!! We have big plans for Christmas gifts this year!" – Steve & Trudy Osborn, Garland, TX

"Thank you so much.... I've already read a good bit of your book – you explain things very clearly. And I really appreciate the enhancing material: history, symbolism, etc. The book does an excellent job of suggesting a wide variety of ways that a fountain can express one's creativity and personality. I'm going to be spending tomorrow 'shopping' in my yard for beautiful stones." – Cindy Bartorillo, Fairfax Station, VA

Create Your Indoor Fountain:

The guide that's launching thousands of fountains!

Create Your Indoor Fountain:

Expressions of the Self

Paris Mannion, LCSW, Professional Coach

Paris Mannion, LCSW
P. O. Box 632864
San Diego, CA 92163
1-800-828-5967
Email: paris@buildfountains.com
http://www.buildfountains.com

Publisher: Paris Mannion
Cover and book design: Tanya A. Inman, tanya@inmandesign.com
Illustrations © Paris Mannion
Photos ©1999 Tanya A. Inman except as noted

Copyright June 1998 by Paris Mannion
second edition, July 1999

Printed in Canada

Library of Congress Card Number 98-96635, 1998
Mannion, Paris, 1941-
    Create Your Indoor Fountain: Expressions of the Self
    Includes bibliography and index
    1. How-To – Crafts 2. Fountain history and symbolism
    3. Fountain feng shui 4. Fountain alchemy
    5. Fountain resources and supplies

ISBN 0-9667102-0-7 (pbk.)

Table of Contents

Foreword

Dr. Katherine R. O'Connell

Some things can surely be considered classics. Fountains are among them. Ever since man developed the small populated clusters that eventually mushroomed into the great city states like Athens and Rome, people have opted consistently to be near the water. If water wasn't close enough to hear its soothing music, we created ways to collect it and present water artfully. Some ancient myths even have humans heading into the ocean water in order to escape a great Atlantean earthquake and eventually taking the form of dolphins, perhaps explaining our closeness in communication with both water and marine mammals.

Not so long after this primordial adventure humans figured out that there were as many purposes for water as there were ways to distribute it. Aqueducts and other forms of piped and channeled water gave rising cities a way to distinguish between and among the various qualities and applications for aqua vitae, the water of life -- public baths and fountains, private garden fountains and grottoes. The Greeks, borrowing many ideas from the Egyptians, held certain bodies of water to be sacred. These sacred lakes were known for their healing properties, and special techniques were designed to carry this water into the ancient sites of healing. The dream incubation Temple of Hathor in Egypt and the Æsclepian Temple in Greece are two healing sites among many.

But why did people go out of their way to obtain this special water? And furthermore what did they do with this healing water, and why is this relevant to us today? Until relatively recently this was not well understood; even now we have much to learn about healing water. Greater study will very likely shine more light on how ancient healing practices worked.

As a result of research I have conducted on ancient medicine and dream healing, I can offer this explanation. The sacred water was piped into the temple and was directed to flow over specially selected stones, carefully and deliberately placed in a cluster in the sacred fountain. As Ms. Mannion notes in her book, the fountain represents access to hidden springs and sources; water gushing forth is a symbol of the life force. The physicians at the temples went to this special effort because they recognized that stones have very specific healing properties.

When the water hit the stones as it flowed over them, a healing vapor was released. When inhaled, the vapor was immediately distributed throughout the body, acting as a pharmacologically potent healing substance. Breathing in a gaseous or vaporous substance is still the most powerful and quickest way to obtain optimal effects of any active substance. At that time much was known about the healing properties of water and stone and how their energy grew when combined. Our own modern medicine could benefit from more of this knowledge.

These ancient fountains, then, were a powerful source of healing energy. The popularity of indoor fountains is growing today just as other forms of energetic medicine are experiencing peaks of interest: homeopathy, flower and gem remedies, aroma therapy, feng shui, crystal healing and even "the Mozart effect" on brain waves. Fountains are more than a bowl, stones, and a pump, or even a lovely appendage. Indoor springs carry potential healing effects when the properties of water and stone are studied and experimented with. As a matter of fact the healing vapor from the fountain water was so potent that people coming to the Egyptian dream temples were instructed to sleep there for three nights; before sleeping they were to ask the Goddess Isis for a healing dream as this was her specialty. In the dream, Isis healed in three ways: by giving information and healing prescriptives; by giving helpful guidance for someone else's healing if it were asked; and most significantly, by healing directly through the dream itself.

Rituals like the fountain creation were an important part of the fabric of Egyptian cosmology, their theory of the origin of the universe. While crafting a fountain, an individual might invoke the personal deities that protect and guide his or her life. *Create Your Indoor Fountain* offers many wonderful examples of ritual objects that can be used in a fountain.

From this we can see how our appreciation of fountains is considerably deepened if we are aware now of ancient medicine and ritual. To prepare a fountain is truly a recreational activity in the original sense of the word. Re-creation is a process where we reinvent ourselves and co-create with the great creator our own life and world. Ms. Mannion's training as a personal coach is invaluable here in helping us focus on what we actually do want in our lives. Her provocative questions may catch you off guard and get you thinking.

The Egyptians believed that their world was in effect recreated every day and that careful attention to nature and to our dreams literally kept the heavens and earth in right order, harmonious with each other. As Ms. Mannion points out, feng shui from China is also a method of balancing the energies of wind and water to ensure right order and harmony.

This book was written with great expertise and love for the subject by an extraordinary woman who combines personal experience, professional training, and an inquisitive mind. She presents this richly illustrated book to you so you may have another tool to exert a positive influence on your environment, moods, and inner self. Books like hers and others in her bibliography carry with them a reminder of the rich lineage we are left by our ancestors. The act of putting together a pleasing and expressive fountain with awareness of its meaning helps keep alive this connection to earth and to spirit. And that is what both re-creation and fountains are all about

Rev. Dr. Katherine R. O'Connell

Capitola, CA
Email: kathleen@got.net
July 20, 1999

About the Author

 Paris Mannion, LCSW and Certified Professional Coach, studied two years at the C. G. Jung Institute in Zurich, Switzerland, exploring many symbols of alchemy, or transformation. Chief among these symbols is the fountain (the source of the "living water") surrounded by the garden (the temenos or sacred space). Paris later researched feng shui, the ancient Chinese art of placement. Moving water increases harmony, balance, and the flow of ch'i (energy, prosperity) in our environment. Increased awareness of our environment can lead to greater self-awareness overall, and here's where coaching comes in.

Coaching uses a process of inquiry and personal discovery to build the client's level of awareness and responsibility, and move into action. Combining coaching questions with the traditions of alchemy and feng shui, Paris now offers a unique opportunity for you to use your hands to effect change in your surroundings, spur personal transformation, and create a beautiful gift for yourself. Because you arrange the fountain garden and select the finishing touches, no two creations are the same. Crafting your fountain garden is a reminder of our connection with nature as well as a connection to an inner self, a blend of ancient wisdom and future science.

For over 2 years Paris was a featured workshop leader at the Learning Annex in San Francisco and Los Angeles, teaching fountain enthusiasts as they craft their personal fountains. Since 1995 she has led classes in California at community colleges, adult eduction centers, and recreation centers.

Acknowledgements

Many have contributed to this edition of Create Your Indoor Fountain. From the demonstration audiences and class participants, I heard helpful questions and suggestions that guided me in this revision. In particular I thank Glenn Harrison (Downey, CA) at Table Top Fountains for technical assistance. He and Randall Reid (Half Moon Bay, CA), potter, are master fountain craftsmen, known for their quality work and courteous manner. Susan Picklesimer (San Francisco) at Fountain Heads and Carol Lorraine (Half Moon Bay, CA), Visionary Coach, shared tips and creative ideas with me.

Tanya A. Inman (Sunnyvale, CA), graphic artist, desktop publisher, and photographer, took many of the photos used here. Judith Cohen (Berkeley, CA), writing coach, asked me questions that helped shape a more coherent text so that "the water flow is not stalled". Dr. Michael Sweeney (Santa Clara University, CA), chemistry professor, consulted with me on negative ions. Dr. Sally Scully (San Francisco State University), Renaissance historian, consulted with me on facts and sequence. June Singer, Jungian analyst, smoothed and clarified some rough edges. My dear friends Ian and Catherine gave me the boost I needed.

My thanks to all. Responsibility for the finished product is mine.

How to Use This Book

Dear Readers,

Start at Part B if you are ready to jump in with both feet. On your way to Part B, on page 79, flip through the early part to look at the pictures for design ideas and context to use when you get to Part B.

Or else start at Part A. Reading this section will enhance your ability to make fountains. I wrote this section to give breadth and depth to the subject of indoor fountains. Most crafts books don't include a "library" section. But here creators of fountains will find the inspiration and boldness to experiment with different designs and discover their fountain style.

Create Your Indoor Fountain incorporates some great fountain images and designs. Let them inspire you. Build on them and be more creative, drawing on old models and fountains' historical use. You can create a fountain that doesn't look like mine but expresses your own tastes.

Even when building fountains I am still first and foremost a coach committed to helping people create the life they desire. I incorporate coaching questions, especially in the first section, so that you may use the book for maximum benefit.

Be open to the idea of actually answering the questions and doing the work. It will help you create a fountain with the greatest value, get clearer on your life, and actually build a fountain for the use intended.

I used questions in this section of the book because questions, in coaching, are how clients learn. These questions promote your learning about yourselves, what you're looking for in a fountain, and why fountains have a magnetic appeal.

Write in the margins, inside front and back cover, or in a journal. Let the creativity flow!

Paris Mannion

Paris Mannion, LCSW
Coach and Fountaineer

Tiny, 2" high porcelain philosophers discuss the merits of life in a fountain setting.

Introduction

Hello, greetings and welcome to the fascinating world of indoor fountain gardens! The surge of interest in table top fountains as a stress-reducer comes at a time when many of us feel too busy, pressured, and out of balance. My book has two purposes: to guide you step by step in crafting your fountain, and to provoke further exploration into personal growth.

Through time people have been attracted to the soothing sound of flowing water, which seems to wear away the cares of the day. Water produces an endless range of sounds as it flows over and around obstructions. In some traditional doctrines, sound is considered the first of all things created, that which gave rise to everything else. Let us see how we can produce these natural healing sounds for ourselves.

What is a Fountain Garden?

Fountains are spouts to channel water under pressure for decorative and cooling effects. Persian paradise gardens of the thirteenth century displayed fountains, channels and waterfalls. These uses of water developed from the irrigation channels and reflective pools of Egypt and Babylon. The pools reflected shady trees, fragrant flowers, and garden foliage–an earthly paradise.

Today, we can recreate these and other effects. A submersible pump (about 2 square inches) is placed in a container at least 2" deep and 6" to 20" wide. The pump spout is fitted with plastic tubing to elevate the water, and the water flow regulator is set on low. Then tap water is added to the container and the pump is plugged into a socket. Water flows upward from the tubing and is recirculated in the container below through the pump's intake valve. Stones, plants and flowers are added to the fountain container, as well as accents such as crystals, statues, shells, incense, and candles.

The water pourer, Aquarius. From the zodiac of Dendera.

15

The Spring of Life, Stone relief. Venice c. 9-10th century.

The result is a sensory experience that anchors us in the present, bringing in relaxation, discovery, and creativity.

Why Would I Want a Fountain Garden?

In our approach to fountain gardens, we have asked these questions:

What historic and symbolic significance do fountains have?

The significance of fountain symbolism lies in its connection to water and to gardens. Water symbolizes the abundance of possibilities and, with sound, the primal origin of all being. Water is identified with intuitive wisdom, which precedes form and creation.

The garden in which water flows is a symbol of earthly and heavenly paradise and of the cosmic order. The garden represents consciousness, as opposed to the forest, the unconscious, where things grow wild.

The fountain with water gushing forth is a symbol of the life-force. In Chapter 1 we discuss fountains in history, surveying Eastern, Mid-Eastern, and European expressions.

How can a fountain garden promote healing?

Fountains circulate positive energy or ch'i, especially when placed according to feng shui principles. This ancient Chinese art is a carefully thought out philosophy that guides us in balancing the natural forces of wind and water for a harmonious and peaceful environment.

Fountains also release negative ions, thought to promote better moods, concentration, and sleep. The so-called "happy ions" predominate near moving water – seashores, waterfalls, and, to a lesser degree, indoor fountains.

In Chapter 2 we will explore feng shui and negative ions in more detail.

How is making a fountain garden an act and symbol of creation?

All creation is an awakening toward consciousness. In creation myths, man becomes aware of himself as a thinking and feeling creature. The process of creation unfolds as we compose a fountain, selecting this piece and rejecting that, experimenting, experiencing moods of satisfaction and frustration, and seeking a new balance. In Chapter 3 we will explore creation themes and trace the psychological implications of the creative act.

A loving couple standing in the Fountain of Life. © Nova Development.

How is the fountain garden an artistic expression?

The ancient practice of alchemy[1] now has a modern guise – indoor fountains. The fountain garden can be a tool for transformation, a tool that has an outward artistic expression as well as a parallel inner process. In Chapter 4 we will see how sixteenth century alchemists represented their symbolic fountains and what the fountain meant to them.

How else can a fountain be used?

Desire for the sound of rippling, murmuring water seems to be the number one reason people want fountains. In addition to creating a peaceful, natural indoor environment, fountain builders want to augment or create an altar, give a unique gift, use the fountain as a meditation tool, or run it at night as a sleep aid and room humidifier.

In doctors and dentists' offices, low maintenance indoor fountains are slowly replacing higher maintenance aquariums. Those in the helping professions (such as therapists, acupuncturists, chiropractors, and masseurs) also find a gentle fountain is relaxing for their clients. Desktop fountains at the workplace provide a white noise and calming visual effect that facilitate clear thinking and improved communication.

Can I build a fountain easily?

A fountain garden is easy and fun to build. In chapters 4 through 7, we review the materials needed, assembly steps, accenting suggestions, and maintenance of the fountain. The Appendix includes a symbols dictionary which offers insight into the universal meaning of the accents we choose.

I hope you will find your fountain garden as exciting and satisfying to make and enjoy as I have. Best wishes!

Abalone shell with water flowing past a blossom onto green malachite below, with amethyst point, starfish, and airplant.

Zen meditation fountain with black slate and smooth stones, and airplant.

Rocks have been pulled away to reveal the pump supporting a drilled African pagoda stone. Water flows down the stone face and recirculates in this freeform glazed turquoise and copper dish. Student composition, San Francisco Learning Annex, 2/98. Photo © Paris Mannion.

A bamboo water chute rests over the pump spout, with pebbles, plants, turquoise accents. The bamboo chute is available at some garden stores. Student composition, San Francisco Learning Annex 3/98. Photo © Paris Mannion

Chapter 1: Fountains in History

Water

Water has played a significant part in tradition and emotion almost everywhere civilization has developed. Man's dependence on water for life is symbolized in most creation myths. Water has a complex range of meanings.

As an unformed, undifferentiated mass, water symbolizes the abundance of possibilities which precede form and creation. Water represents the primal origin of all being, the first matter from which life springs. Its qualities of transparency and depth are also associated with the transition between fire and air (ethereal) and earth (material). Spiritual fertility and spiritual life are often represented by water. Water is also identified with intuitive wisdom, natural life, and spiritual cleansing.

Water's mystical powers were particularly revered in cultures where water or the lack of it was of central concern – in the Near East and around the Mediterranean basin. Judaeo-Christian and Islamic religions share the belief in an original Paradise garden. The secure and ever-lasting garden is home to the four rivers of life which flow to the different regions of the earth.[2] Will you create a Paradise Garden with your fountain?

Water produces an endless range of sounds as it flows over and around obstructions. While the earliest springs are natural springs, the artificial harnessing of water power for irrigation, sound, and sanctuary dates back to the first Egyptian (Fig. 1) and Babylonian civilizations.

...when there was only water, the sweet water Apsu and the salt water Timet; they mingled together.
– Babylon

River: The four rivers of paradise. After an Alsatian miniature, 12th century.

In ancient Greece and Rome springs and water were revered as a source of life, the origin of abundance, virtue, and intellectual life. Water has the power to fructify, purify, and renew in both the mystical and the physical sense. The healing temple of the great Æsculapius was situated near sacred water; the vapors released healing energy.

*Figure 1
The garden pool surrounded by trees is an example of the Egyptian aspective convention, c. 1350-1300 B.C. (E. Wilson, 1986, Fig 5.)*

The worship of Venus seems to have been established in Rome at an early time (114 BC). Venus was originally a Latin goddess said to have sprung from the foam of the sea or to be the daughter of Jupiter and Dione, goddess of moisture. Jupiter-Zeus in the form of a swan, a water bird, lands for a visit with the graceful Leda (Fig. 2) as she regards a lion spurting water. In the Graeco-Roman tradition, river gods were often personified as men holding a cornucopia or horn of plenty, a symbol of fertility and abundance. How would a cornucopia overflowing with water look in your fountain garden? What would that say about your life?

In the far East, too, water was the essence of life. The fifth century BC Chinese philosopher Lao Tsu observes:[3]

*Æsculapius with
staff and serpent.*

"The supreme good is like water,
  which nourishes all things without trying to.
  . . . it is like the Tao."
"Nothing in the world
  is as soft and yielding as water.
  Yet for dissolving the hard and inflexible,
  nothing can surpass it."
"Whoever is soft and yielding
  is a disciple of life.
  The hard and stiff will be broken.

Thou givest [mankind] to drink from the river of thy delights. For with thee is the fountain of life...
–Psalm 36

I will give to him that is a thirst of the fountain of the water of life freely. –Revelation 21:6

In the beginning one of the gods of heaven stirred the chaotic waters with his staff...
– Japan

Figure 2
Leda from the Quattro Fontaine, Rome.

The soft and simple will prevail."
"Do you have the patience to wait
til your mud settles and the water is clear?"

Gardens

In the East Asian garden, little imposes on nature's setting. Gentle waterfalls, quiet streams, and pools surround pavilions that shimmer in reflecting light, a synthesis of natural elements (Fig. 3). Water provides fluidity, sound and motion;

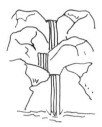

Three step broken fall.

Figure 3
Here the stream is shallow so that the small stones in the bed are visible and become part of the design. Hammered in posts with lilies support the bank. The flat rock can be used for sitting (after Seike, et al, 1980).

these qualities offset the immobility and heaviness of purposefully arranged stones and rocks. One part of nature represents something else. A rock, for instance, symbolizes an entire mountain; or a chrysanthemum blossom represents the quality of beauty. What symbols will you select for your fountain garden?

In some Eastern gardens, the elements – stone, water and plant – are balanced to suggest quiet and repose. The gardener's design is complete when there's nothing more to be removed from the garden, and the garden has something of the panoramic appearance of a natural view.[4]

Random fall.

In other Eastern gardens, moving water provides a vital focus. The waterfall is an important motif

Figure 4
Miniature waterfall seen from different viewpoints.

Single fall.

in Japanese and Chinese landscape painting. Its plunging downward is seen as the opposite of the upward striving cliff or rock. The waterfall (Yin) is considered to represent the opposite of the cliff's immobility (Yang). The waterfall has a seemingly constant form which endures the continual change of the flowing water. In Buddhism a waterfall is a symbol of the insubstantiality of everything worldly.

Fountain cascading from a central spout.

The composition looks best when the source of water is visible. Consider the various viewpoints from which the waterfall will be seen. The waterfall can be angled to enhance a particular aspect or accent of your fountain garden. In a larger bowl, the waterfall fountain can be built as a single fall, a three-tiered broken fall, or a random fall.

Or you might hide the waterfall with various plants to reveal it from another viewpoint. (Fig. 4) Increase the surprise.

Waterfalls bring water to life by their ever changing display of splashing and murmuring. These sounds need to be integrated into the design. Lower the pumps' water regulator if using a waterfall in a contemplative indoor space or in a bedroom.

Sand can also be raked to give the impression of moving water (Fig. 5). In the fifteenth and sixteenth centuries, water features like seas and waterfalls came to be represented by stone and gravel alone, simple and provocative as Zen

Figure 5

Raking sand into ripple patterns gives the "sea" great turbulence. Miniature hills suggest a coastal mountain range (after Seike, et al, 1980).

Buddhism. Gradually the laying out of gardens became crystallized in the principles of feng shui. Feng shui is the art of placing and balancing the elements of wind and water for harmonious surroundings.

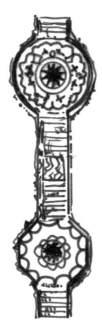

In Italy, pleasure gardens for a cool, refreshing retreat first appeared in the second century BC. Hellenistic trading settlements along the Italian coast imported Greek artists; their work strongly influenced the Roman arts. Excavations of Hadrian's Villa at Tivoli (2nd c. AD) revealed a large garden with elaborate waterworks, including one fountain that cascaded down a semicircular series of steps.[5] The water stairway or cascade was a popular theme in Renaissance Italy and in Spain (Fig. 6). Perhaps this is an effect you would like to create in your fountain garden. How is your energy flowing?

Figure 6
This bird's eye view shows the plan and section of the Water Staircase at Alhambra, Grenada, Spain.

In the Middle East, gardens have been important retreats from the intensely hot desert environment. In designing a cool and serene sanctuary in a fertile valley, Persian landscapers incorporated powerful religious symbolism. The Persian or paradise garden is divided into two crossed axes. The quadrants symbolize the belief that the universe is divided by the four great rivers of life.

The watercourse garden recreates the original paradise. High walls, trees, shrubs and brilliant floral borders create a shady oasis.[6] (Fig. 7). Irrigation provides formal pools to reflect the nature around it while gentle dripping fountains add a musical dimension to the contemplative setting.

Vertical water stairway at the Villa d'Este, Campania, Italy.

26

A paradise garden (Fig. 8) might be created using a square bowl about 2 1/2" deep with the pump centered and the bowl filled level with small dark pebbles. Contrasting white pebbles can trace the quadrants, and flower stems or plant cuttings decorate the edges. What is your idea of heaven on earth?

Figure 7
This backyard California garden shows Near Eastern influence: ground level water channels and square pools with center fountain jet.

The main difference between Eastern and Western gardens is scale. In the gardens of China and Japan, the goal is the recreation of nature in miniature. The effect is serenity, balance and asymmetry. In the West, control over nature is more pronounced and symmetrical and the scale is grand.

Figure 8
A tiny bit of paradise. A small brass plumbing fixture just fits over the pump spout to elevate the water about an inch. Photo © Paris Mannion.

Fountains

Fountains are spouts to channel water under pressure for decorative and cooling effects. Throughout history, fountains have been important features of cities, gardens and private houses. The Fontana Maggiore in Perugia, Italy (1278), was the first to exploit the decorative effect of water cascading from a central spout.

In addition to decorating the villas and gardens of wealthy Romans, fountains served the practical function in cities as sources of public baths and water supply, a central gathering space. They still do today. Survivors of San Francisco's 1906 earthquake gathered on April 18, 1998 at Lotta's

Plan of Taj-Mahal gardens.

Figure 9
Octagonal fountain of the Domus Flavia, Rome.

Figure 10
Oval fountain of the Domus Flavia, Rome.

Fountain to commemorate the moment the earthquake struck. The fountain was a rallying point after the quake. Survivors went there to find their loved ones 92 years ago.[7]

Graeco-Roman Influence

One of the few remaining fountain structures from classical times are found in the Palatine, a section of Rome. Built about 81 AD, one fountain of Domus Flavia is octagonal in shape (Fig. 9). It appears that water flowed from a higher to lower level, spreading out along four banks. Another fountain of Domus Flavia is the oval fountain, designed to be seen from above, from the dining hall of the palace. (Fig. 10).

Poetic sources from Greece and Rome contain many references to fountains, water, nature

Detail of Domus Flavia Octagon showing sloping channels.

Figure 11
Fountain with naturalistic backdrop in Rome. Photo ©
Paris Mannion.

springs, and grottoes. The dominant poetic image from classical times was naturalistic, with rocky caves, tumbling streams, woodland lakes. Figure 11 shows a modern variant on this fountain theme with the woodland decor built up along the wall of the house and a water spout toward the front of the basin.

For many fountains, water was stored in a reservoir built behind a wall or niche and trickled down when the rocky, naturalistic fountain was turned on. We can recreate this gentle dripping by setting the pump on low. How would a naturalistic backdrop look for your fountain? What will soothe you and recharge your batteries?

Springs, the "source of Poetry", were associated with the Muses who inspired all intellectual activ-

A Roman aqueduct.
Image © Nova
Development.

Ceres (Minerva) by Ammannati. Florence, 16th c. marble statue; water flows from her breasts when fountain is turned on.

ity. The spring at Delphi conferred the power to foretell the future, while the waters of Lethe offered oblivion to those who entered the underworld. Water introduces an element of forgetfulness; it dissolves fixed outlines, loosens the knot of experience, and carries the past away. Will your indoor spring dissolve a fixed perspective or loosen things up so something new may develop?

This intellectual interaction with water in the past "Golden Age" was rediscovered in fifteenth and sixteenth century Italy. The technology was rediscovered also. Renaissance Italy architects, engineers and sculptors collaborated in building water works that used steam, differential pressure, pulleys and hydrostatic principles that originated with the Greeks many centuries earlier.[8]

Over time rich associations developed for water, fountain, spring and source. For "spring" in the Oxford English Dictionary of 1881 are cited Springs of water of grace, springs of life, Fame's immortal spring, and Ovid, the spring and well of poets. For "fountain" the list includes the Fountain of Honor, fountains of trust, and Fountain of Justice[9], something that springs clean from the source. What do you associate with fountains? How will you represent this association?

Persian-Islamic Influence

Water dissolves fixed outlines and loosens the knot of experience. Image © Nova Development.

With the end of the Crusades in 1290, Moorish or Muslim influence in European art and literature really began. Starting in the late Middle Ages (about 1350 AD), a steady flow of Italian travelers visited Islamic centers along the coast of North Africa. Travelers also set out inland from the coast of modern Israel. Many arrived at the courts of the Baghdad Caliphate and the Persian Shahs; some reached the western part of India. A varied group of ambassadors, merchants, missionaries and adventurers returned with vivid descriptions of the courtyards they had visited, praising the fountains and pavilions.

Figure 12
Arching jets, quiet water; Tivoli, Italy.

A common feature of Persian gardens picked up in Renaissance Italy was a sloped water chute with a textured surface to break the water flow into a turbulent pattern. Water lighting was used in the Mogul gardens of Persia and in Italian Renaissance fountains. The theme of arching water jets crossing along an axis was picked up by Renaissance landscape architects, showing water in repose and water in motion (Fig. 12). If you were like water, when would you be in repose and in motion?

Arching jets for your indoor fountain can be made by perforating flexible tubing attached to the pump's spout and laying it horizontally or curved in the container. A miniature water jet attachment is also available for the pump spout. The unusual effect resembles a lawn sprinkler in a garden setting. Be sure the bowl is big enough to contain the splash. Where might you place a light? How might a sloped water chute with textured surface look in your fountain? What breaks your flow into a turbulent pattern?

Islamic influence in Spain can today be seen in the magnificent Moorish gardens at Seville or Granada (Fig.13) where water dominates in the form of shimmering, narrow pools and numerous arching jets. Shrubs in pots and box hedges line the pool edges and reflect the natural environ-

Detail of water chute in shell, or pigeon breast, pattern. Somewhat resembles a cheese grater with a solid back.

Adaptation of the ancient water staircase to a modern tabletop fountain.

ment. Later fountain architects added cascades, dynamic forms that dramatize human control over nature.

Renaissance Fountains

Figure 13
Pool with Arching Water Jets, Alhambra, Grenada, Spain (after MacDougall, 1978, VI, 6).

Many ancient statues unearthed near Rome were in frontal or horizontal poses, suitable for installation in a wall niche (Fig. 14). Here the lady stands above a lion's head from which water flows to the oblong basin below. She is one of three such fountains along the garden wall.

The early sixteenth century fountains belonging to humanists of the Papal court reflect the poetic image from classical times. Their garden fountains were naturalistic, with rocky caves, tumbling streams, and woodland lakes. The mood was nostalgic. One garden outside Rome near St. Peter's belonged to Blosius Palladius. He had it built on a terraced hillside with fountains and pools on each level. At the garden entrance a fountain was surrounded by marble benches shaded by laurel trees. Beyond, a slope was planted with lemon trees; at the top of the slope was a terrace where dinners were held. A fountain in the center of the terrace was shaded by a latticed arbor with grape vines.[10]

A craggy rock-hewn face looks over the countryside at the Villa d'Este, Campania, Italy.

Figure 14
Wall fountain at the Medici Gardens, Rome. Photo © Paris Mannion.

A similar scene in miniature might be created by terracing flat rocks along the sides of a large bowl to build up height at the back. Then the water can be diverted by a "Y" device into two streams to run down the stones and into a pool. Place a miniature bench (from an aquarium or oriental store) and silk plants or moss in the foreground or add a miniature latticed arbor with vines.

Gurgling mask at the terminus of a water staircase, Villa d'Este, Campania, Italy.

Because fountains set the mood and pleased the senses, they often became the subject of poems. Water seems to speak to the imagination because it bears a flowing image. "Speaking water" ripples and murmurs over stone; "reflecting water" lies in the pool below. Attending to the voice of a fountain, the poet was often led to commune with his or her own inwardness. How do you find your natural rhythm?

Fountains and the decorations associated with water[11] were often the focus of the garden design. The fountains, pools, and grottoes provided the vehicle for the narrative and allegorical context of the garden's theme. What is the theme for your fountain garden?

Grottoes are cave-like enclosures formed from artificial or natural caves (Fig. 15). These caves were designed to stimulate intellectual activity (through the influence of Apollo and the Muses) and the appreciation of water as benefactor, fructifier, and life giver (with statues of the healer Æsculapius). A miniature fountain grotto can be built with an underwater light inside the "cave" to highlight water flowing. The grotto itself can be built by layering flat stones on either side of the entrance. The pump spout can be at the cave entrance or further into the cave. What aspect of your personality would a grotto suggest? What work would you do in a grotto?

*Figure 15
Grotto at the Villa d'Este, Campania.*

Detail of water fan in grotto of Figure 15.

Figure 16
Oval Fountain, Villa d'Este, Campania, Italy.

In the sixteenth century, immense series of cascades and waterfalls were constructed at the Villa d'Este, situated on a hilltop near Rome (Fig. 16). These waterfalls were possible because of the powerful nearby Aniene River which starts in the mountains. Lower-lying cities such as Rome had not the water pressure to create huge waterfalls.

However, a great change occurred in fountain design at the end of the sixteenth century as the result of the construction of the Acqua Felice. This aqueduct for the first time since antiquity provided a plenteous water supply with adequate pressure. The movement and sound of water could now be controlled, and sculptural form could be imposed upon the water itself. Waterfalls could now be created, and waterfall fountains soon became popular in Rome and elsewhere. How would a waterfall look in your fountain? When are you like the water, plunging downward? Or like the rock or cliff, striving upward?

Water spills from a mask along the Avenue of 100 Fountains, Villa d'Este, Italy.

During the Age of Louis XIV, the Baroque Gardens of Versailles, with their geometric plans, clipped shrubbery and soaring jets of water, symbolized man's dominion over nature. Concepts of the mathematical ideal and the perfectibility of Nature signaled the modern Scientific Revolution and foreshadowed the Enlightenment which followed.

Paradoxically, it is through scientific discoveries, such as the harnessing of electricity and invention of submersible pumps, that we have a convenient way to reconnect with nature. With a table top fountain we can also counteract the damaging effects of modern technology such as air pollution and traffic noise. By bringing a fountain indoors, we create a more harmonious environment with cleaner, healthier air and calming sound.

Aqueduct: The end point or terminus of an aqueduct near Pirimide Station, Rome.

Water spouts from small hole in a green marble egg (foreground), with irregular driftwood pieces and airplant. Robert Birnbach, photographer; Susan Picklesimer, artist (415-921-7902).

Incense plumes delicately above a contented jade wayfarer as he contemplates the spring before him.

Chapter 2:
The Fountain as an Environmental Healer

Feng Shui

We may recall that feng shui principles grew out of meditation in the tea garden. By reconnecting with natural elements such as water, stones and plants, we can be revitalized by the subtle currents of life force and beauty that flow through the landscape. The landscape might be the natural outdoors, the miniature Asian tea garden, or an indoor fountain set as a tea garden.

Feng shui in today's terms means using our environment in a positive way to create a healthy, prosperous life and minimize the damaging effects of environmental pollutants. According to feng shui experts, there are solutions or "cures" for difficulties in life, difficulties made worse by our often over-stressed, sleep deprived life styles.

Feng shui is the Chinese art of placement to bring harmony and balance to the environment. The placement refers to arranging objects to add energy to our lives – the furnishing of home or office, the use of property or lot, the planting of trees and plants, as well as the use of water and nature. Using water, wind, and nature in a fountain garden is a powerful feng shui cure.

The origins of feng shui date back several millennia. By the fourth century BC, the Chinese elite consulted shamans to determine the proper placement of homes, pathways and temples. They sought areas where the elements, especially wind (feng) and water (shui), were in harmony. A home, for instance, would offer its occupants a

Chinese character for Feng Shui.

A house facing a waterfall brings good fortune.

"Water never rests, neither by day nor by night..." Photo © Nova Development.

more pleasant life if it were near a source of fresh water and protected from harsh winds. This common sense approach to building occurs in most cultures, in the general sense of relating with the Earth as sacred space.

The specific rules and practices currently identifiable as feng shui seem to date to the fourteenth and fifteenth centuries, when garden principles were formulated into rules of placement. Feng shui contains the basic elements of Chinese thought: the Tao, the theory of yin-yang, and Chinese astrology.[12]

Lao-tsu, Taoist philosopher of fifth century China, writes of the physical and spiritual water:[13]

> "Water never rests, neither by day nor by night.
> When flowing above, it causes rain and dew.
> When flowing below, it forms streams and rivers....
> ..it does not struggle
> And yet it has no equal in destroying that which is strong and hard."

The watercourse way represented in a fountain garden is an invitation to blend and not struggle, to flow with life, and endure continual change. What is it to do this in life? How can we stay centered enough to flow?

Yin-Yang expresses the two counterbalancing tendencies of materialization and spiritualization. A symbolic expression of yin-yang is the waterfall, an important motif in Chinese landscape painting and gardens. The waterfall (yin) plunging downward is seen as the opposite of the upward striving, immobile rock (yang). A fountain waterfall is a reminder of continual change (water), although the form seems constant (rocks) – a symbol of the unsubstantially of everything worldly. What is your attitude toward the material world?

The zodiac in Chinese astrology depicts the process of primordial energy becoming fertile, moving from unity to multiplicity, from potential to virtual, from spirit to matter, and then returning along the same path. The twelve zodiac animals might be arranged beneath a year tree in a fountain setting (Fig. 17). What is your zodiac animal?

Figure 17

The Chinese Year has twelve zodiac animals. Pictured is the Dragon. Fortunate is he or she upon whom the Water Dragon smiles.

The other Chinese zodiac animals are:
Rat, Ox, Tiger, Rabbit, Snake, Horse, Ram, Monkey, Cock, Dog, and Pig.

Feng, Chinese for "wind", refers to moving air. This motion is associated with the cosmic breath or "ch'i" that animates all of nature. Ch'i is the force that links man and his surroundings and is also known as the human spirit and universal energy. Shui, Chinese for "water", refers to the source of life. Water symbolizes terrestrial and natural life; limitless and immortal, water is the beginning and the end of all things on earth.

In Chinese philosophy, man's role is to maintain harmony among wind and water, and the three other elements of metal, fire, and earth. An indoor fountain garden might contain the five elements, symbolizing the desire to maintain balance in one's affairs (Fig. 18).

Different kinds of ch'i circulate in the earth, in the atmosphere and in our bodies. The feng shui practitioner works with all three types of ch'i. Feng shui can be thought of as "environmental acupuncture" because it regulates atmospheric and earthly ch'i the way acupuncture regulates the flow of ch'i in the human body.

The Ba-gua

Another philosophical ingredient in feng shui is the I Ching, from which the Ba-gua, or eight-sided template, is derived. The ancient Chinese book of divination, the I Ching, contains sixty-

Figure 18
The five elements in a fountain: flame of copper oil lamp,
driftwood and plants, bubbling water stirring air.

four hexagrams which map the energy patterns
between heaven, earth, and mankind. The hexagrams are made up of eight trigrams. A trigram is
a group of three lines, either solid or broken.

When the eight trigrams are arranged in a circle,
they form the ba-gua or template. This template
represents the eight directions as well as eight areas in a person's life. The eight areas are: career,
knowledge, family and health, wealth, fame,
marriage, children and creativity, and benefac-
tors or helpful people (Figure 19).

Chinese Yin-Yang,
surrounded by the
eight trigrams.

The Ba-gua template can be imposed on a house,
a room, a desk or conference table, or even on top
of city plans. In the Black Hat sect of feng shui,
the position of the Ba-gua is determined by the location of the door (or front of desk). The "career"
position aligns with the wall from which the
main door opens. Figure 18 illustrates the eight
sides representing eight aspects of one's life.

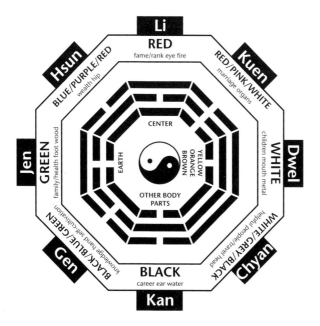

Figure 19
The Five Element Ba-gua Color Wheel. Career (black) po-
sition aligns with the door wall. If the door is left or right
of center, one enters from the knowledge or benefactor
area respectively.

Feng shui is said to harness and enhance environmental ch'i. This channeling improves the flow of energy in our living and working spaces as well as in our bodies, thus improving our life and destiny. Over the centuries, several distinct schools of Chinese feng shui (as well as Korean and Tibetan schools) have evolved. In the last ten years or so, an American style has developed. Its practitioners generally draw on diverse Asian sources, on a sensitivity to the client's needs, and on their own intuition. Described here is the Black Sect Tantric Buddhist tradition of feng shui, including the nine cures and our suggestions for where to place your indoor fountain.

The Nine Cures

The feng shui practitioner may diagnose an over-abundance, an under-abundance, or a stale con-

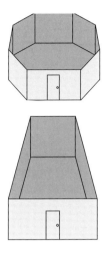

The most auspicious room shapes are octagonal, rectangular, circular, or square.

dition of ch'i in a home or office. He or she can then offer cures that correct that condition. For example, the practitioner might find threatening concentrations of ch'i, such as harsh sunlight, in a room and recommend placing a crystal near the window to disperse the ch'i more evenly.

There are nine basic feng shui cures for achieving the flow of positive energy through a space. A fountain garden can embody all nine of the cures.

Electrically powered objects

Fountain pumps, TV sets, and microwaves can encourage positive ch'i to flow and computers on the left side of a desk generate wealth according to feng shui practitioners. If you place your computer so that you face a door while you work, you will operate from a position of strength and control.

An electrically powered fountain is said to promote wealth, a belief born in times when water was essential to the Chinese economy for its role in the growth of rice. In America we have many associations between water and money. A few are:

- float a loan
- washed up
- money spigot
- frozen assets
- cash flow

A feng shui suggestion is to fix leaks immediately or you may experience money flushed away. Standing water in the bathroom or kitchen can mean a stagnant cash flow. Feng shui practitioners suggest keeping the toilet seat lids down and, when not in use, covering the kitchen drain pipe to prevent "money (water) down the drain".

To encourage business you can place your fountain garden on ether side of the door entrance (door to a room or to the house). This will enhance the *career area* or *career gua* and draw energy enhancing ch'i into the room. On a scale of

1 to 10, how satisfied are you in your career?

Moving objects

Interior fountains are also microcosms of ch'i-activating and money producing water. Flowing water can be protective because it disperses the killing ch'i of design flaws such as jutting angles or a missing ba-gua area.

Wind and water, the creative forces of nature that give feng shui its name, are brought indoors to encourage abundance. A table top fountain might be placed in the *creativity/children gua* to encourage an "offspring" of ideas. Moving air produced by moving water in an indoor fountain captures the essence of feng shui. How will you express your creativity?

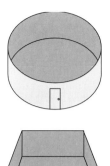

The integrity of regular shapes gives the room's occupant a sense of completeness.

Living objects

Fish bowls and aquariums are smaller versions of the life-giving ocean and evoke nourishing ch'i.

Plants and flowers, too, symbolize life and growth. They breathe a new energy into any interior and help circulate what is already there. Plants in a fountain or alone can smooth out design imbalances such as acute room angles, corners that jut into rooms, or unused storage space. A plant placed under an open staircase at home will draw positive energy to the upstairs area.

A fountain garden can boost performance and morale when placed diagonally to the right of an entrance in the *benefactor gua* because, it is said, helpful people will be attracted. Where will you place your fountain?

Sound

Wind chimes and bells can lure ch'i (and customers) in because they produce noise. Feng shui experts suggest placing a chime or bell in a dark corner or over your bed or desk to attract energy. Ch'i energy enters or leaves buildings through windows. To keep ch'i from leaving a room with many doors or windows, you might add a wind

When applying the Ba-Gua to an irregularly shaped room or house, there will be additions or deficits. An area less than half the room's width or length is considered addition (like the alcove above). An area larger than half creates a deficit in the far corner (below).

Blue, purple, or red

Color can cure a missing area: a room missing the wealth area (upper left) can be fixed by adding something blue, purple or red.

chime or bell to your fountain garden. Give it a jingle now and then.

The bubbling sound of a small indoor fountain might be profitably placed in the *wealth gua*. People are drawn to the natural background noise. How do you measure wealth?

Heavy Objects

Stones, statues, and other weighty items are used to restrain positive ch'i and keep it from leaving a space. Strategically placed in the area of your choice, a heavy object can enhance health, wealth and emotional well-being.

Heavy stones in the fountain bowl placed in the *family gua*, for instance, represent steadfastness and solidity. How are your family relations? Who have you been meaning to call?

Bright Objects

Crystal balls, lights, candles, and mirrors brighten any interior and attract positive energy. Mirrors in a cramped room will make the room seem larger; a mirror placed at right angles to the window will bring the view inside. However, a mirror in front of a bed can disturb your sleep. A crystal hung in the middle of a long corridor can slow down quickly moving ch'i, and lights can soften a sharply jutting corner.

A fountain garden with candle flame or underwater light placed in the *fame gua* will cast a brightness, drawing life, happiness and positive regard. Are you ready to step forward and be noticed?

Colors

Red, symbolizing happiness and strength, is the most auspicious color and is the color most used in feng shui cures. Related colors, such as purple, pink and plum, are also fortunate. Green promotes growth and tranquility; blue can be beneficial or not depending of the shade (warmer and with a hint of green is best). Brown, tan, yellow and orange harmonize a room with the earth.

For more on colors, see the Dictionary of Symbols at the end of the book.

A fountain accented with red birds, rose or clear quartz, and green plants might be placed in the *marriage gua* to draw in harmony and happiness. Do you have an inner marriage as well?

Bamboo Flutes

When hung on a diagonal from the ceiling or on a wall, bamboo flutes symbolize growth, stability and safety, say practitioners. When two flutes, mouth pieces up and tied with red ribbons, are hung on a diagonal from a beam that runs above a stove, desk, or bed, then oppressive energy caused by the beam is dispelled. The flutes symbolically form the ba-gua, which is auspicious.

Bamboo tube for directing the flow of water. Photo © Paris Mannion.

A fountain with a miniature flute placed diagonally on a rock or a hollow bamboo tube through which water flows might be placed in the *knowledge gua* to draw in positive energy and help a student progress in learning. How are you progressing with what you need to learn?

Ribbons, fringes and fragrance

Because feng shui cures evolve and change to address new problems, this category is open to additional ways to increase the flow of positive energy. Red ribbons are tied to "battling doors" with knocking knobs; red tassels can hide and resolve the problem of a slanted beam. How else would you increase the flow of positive energy?

You might place the fountain garden in the gua you wish to enhance. Or place the fountain in an area of architectural imbalance in order to fill out a missing gua. Are you out of balance or missing an area of life?

Professor Lin Yun, a Black Sect Tantric Buddhist, advises using the Three Secrets Reinforcement Technique[14] to activate the solutions for maximum effectiveness. The first technique is placing your hands on the objects, the physical work of moving furniture or hanging pictures. The sec-

Ch'I is the cosmic breath or energy of all beings, the earth, and the atmosphere.

ond involves speech, reciting a mantra or prayer nine times. The third technique is visualization with harmony and balance as stated intent.

In *The Western Guide to Feng Shui: Creating Balance, Harmony and Prosperity in Your Environment* Terah Kathryn Collins summarizes feng shui in the office and home:[15]

• Our home and work environments are vibrantly alive, completely interconnected with the rest of our lives, and subject to change at any time.

• When our choices in selecting and arranging our environments are focused on comfort and safety, and when we surround ourselves with the things that we love, we enhance the circulation of vital ch'i. This approach creates our own personal paradise.

• Our choices in selecting and arranging our environments can be made to balance yin and yang qualities and the five elements, which also enhance the circulation of vital ch'i.

• Our precise choices of the placement of things in our environment can invite people and vital ch'i in, or it can push people and vital ch'i away.

Interior fountains and waterfalls, she notes, are excellent choices for enhancing the ch'i in any *Bagua* in your home or workplace. They are considered especially powerful in the *Wealth* and *Career areas* because of their association with money.

Readers Respond

Seeing what comes next

"I've always wanted a table top fountain of my own," writes Debra Monroe. "But I didn't have time to research where to buy the parts and figure out how to assemble them.... (With the feng shui information) I placed my lovely new fountains in the relationship corners of my living

Water jets and falls in this octagonal lake, Garden of Luxembourg, Paris.

room and bedroom. Although I haven't yet met my soul mate, I do seem to be doing quite a lot more dating than I have in a long time."

Now when the pace of my dating life slows down a bit, I generally wonder if it is time to clean and rearrange the items in my fountain and see what comes next. My next project is is to create a fountain for my office. I'm sure people who come to our offices high atop a San Francisco skyscraper looking for work will find relaxing the comforting trickling sounds the the water. I'll probably place the new fountain n the prosperity corner of our lobby area." – Debra Monroe, Monroe Personnel Service/Temptime, San Francisco, CA.

Disc fountain at Place Jussieu, Paris, France.

Negative Ions

In addition to the gentle sound of water flowing, the fountain garden also releases negative ions. Ionization occurs spontaneously when moving water is present and is particularly high at the beach and around waterfalls. As water hits the sand or rocks, droplets are sheared (the Lenard effect) and negative ions are released. An indoor fountain is a mild negative ion generator (Fig. 20); water is electromagnetic.

Figure 20
Waterfall fountain with water falling off edge of drilled stone slab.

Negative ions, the so-called "good ions" or "happy ions" seem to enhance our mood, energy, libido, and sense of well-being. In addition, negative ions are thought to improve sleep, alertness, concentration, skin condition, healing of wounds, reaction time, and over all immune functions.[16] Negative ions also attach themselves to pollution particles, cleaning the air.

Magic fountain from garden store.

Old Faithful, Yellowstone National Park. It reaches full height with the gentle swish of a fountain. Photo © Nova Development.

Too many positive ions, on the other hand, have debilitating effects. Our industrial environment has upset natural ion levels; many modern practices increase levels of positive ions, such as combustion, synthetic materials, and driving (the friction of air over metal). The air in energy efficient buildings often contains high levels of gas and particulate pollutants, which can produce a condition called "positive ion poisoning." The result is increased levels of tension, irritability, depression, reduced work efficiently, lethargy or headache. The syndrome is also associated with insomnia and increased frequencies of colds and respiratory problems.

A mild negative ion generating fountain can help create an environment in which the body is better able to recover on its own in the face of chemicals, air-borne pollutants and other twentieth century stresses. Breathing in negative ions seems to increase relaxation and help restore the body's natural balance.

A Healing Environment

Responding to a growing trend, in 1995 the Cortesia Sanctuary Project in Oregon (541-343-9544) began inspiring people to create sanctuaries in gardens, workplaces, homes and bedrooms. Across the country people are organizing community gardens. In August, 1996, the San Jose Mercury News profiled four hospitals which created healing outdoor spaces to soothe "the human spirit". Ancient wisdom blends with future science in these progressive hospitals

Parisienne fountain in springtime.

Non Bo landscape miniatures debuted at the Del Mar, CA, Flower and Garden show in 1996. Non Bo landscape miniatures, generally set in water pools, are an art and meditative form unique to Buddhist-influenced Vietnam. The goal is balance, harmony and respect for nature.[17]

Set in a shallow cement tray about 2' x 3' x 3" high, the Non Bo water garden consists first of a mountain made of glued rocks. The artist then plants baby tears, bonsai, miniature junipers, and shrubs in small dirt-filled depressions among the rocks for a naturally green landscape.

The miniaturist adds small houses, bridges, birds, and temples. Finally the water pump is turned on for streams and waterfalls. A fountain fogger may be added so mysterious mist emerges from a cave. These landscape miniatures, a meditative practice done alone, take three to six month to complete and last several years outdoors.

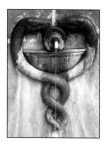

Two snakes form a cadeuseus on this fountain honoring a French pharmicist, Rue Bonaparte, Paris.

Healing can come to the whole organism from restoring and nourishing the body, calming the mind, or connecting with the soul or Self. Healing also can come from being in nature. Or from bringing indoors the soothing, quieting effects of the watercourse way to renew natural sensitivities and uplift our spirits. Reconnecting to nature is important for life balance and long term happiness. A fountain garden is a reminder of our connection with nature as well as a connection to an inner self and an avenue of transformation into something better.

Fountains for Work and Home: Workplace Fountains

Maybe fountains can help sick people, but what about healthy people? How are they benefited by fountains, especially at work? Experience shows that:

- Workplace table top fountains reduce the level of stress.

- The white noise and calming visual effects facilitate clear thinking.

- The soothing sound of moving water sets a tone for creativity and improved communication.

- You can customize your work environment to bring in relaxation, discovery, and productivity.

The water course serpentine is a Near Eastern design with water channels at ground level.

The goddess Kwan Yin in the aspect of a cement garden statue.

Are you and your company prepared for growth? Moving water in China is associated with life, harmony, and especially money. Consider our own associations between water and money:

- cash flow
- liquid assets
- slush fund
- washed up
- bank
- frozen assets
- flush with money
- float a loan
- laundered money
- money down the drain

Aside from the career and money-enhancing possibilities, fountains can be the center of a special place in an office setting. The fountain accents act as visual reminders of the sources of inspiration in the owner's life.[18]

A statue of Athena for invention or a wolf image for leadership can be used to strengthen you. A Kwan Yin figurine (Fig. 21) for compassion or a snake for energy and transformation can keep you focused on qualities you want to incorporate into your working day.

Figure 21
Water flows over shells beside Kwan Yin, goddess of mercy and compassion, with copper oil lamp in background.

The pleasant scent from a flower or pine cone adds to the sensory experience. The fountain objects are available for a bolstering touch. Bright colored accents cast high energy, while soft colors have a calming effect. Sensory development is a low cost way to to increase creativity and productivity and to make changes in relationships, space, and culture.

Smiling Buddhas grace many a fountain.

Readers Respond

Who Knew?

Diane Miner, a reader from Beverly Hills, CA, made a fountain for her office desk. Co-workers "ooh-ed and aah-ed" so much she agreed to make a few more. The office workers felt more relaxed and efficient when they could hear or see Diane's. So Diane started making fountains for sale in her office.

Home Fountains

We have explored some benefits of workplace fountains. What about benefits to your health in your home? These benefits have been reported:

- Cleans the air by the fountain's pulling in particles, lint, dust, pollutants.

- Helps you relaxing into sleep. Why play a sleep aid tape of mountain brooks?

- Calms and refreshes you by bringing nature sounds indoors.

- Increases the positive ch'i of air stirred by water.

- Improves your mood and concentration with its negative ions.

- Lifts your spirits with a visually pleasing sight in the living or sleeping space.

- Inspires your heart and mind when engaged in personal fountain creation.

Black slate fountainhead.

Diana of Ephesus, ruler and nourisher of the celestial beasts of the zodiac.

• Enriches oxygen from newly lush plants near the fountain for fuller breathing.

• Humidifies dry air and gives your nostrils a break.

• Displays a happy "dish of memories" for instant cheer and inspiration.

As a sanctuary, a fountain sets the stage for going within – both physically coming to an attactive water setting and also mentally journeying into one's self. As you change accents, bowls, or location over time, your fountain can serve as a meditation tool to monitor your moods. For example, a rose quartz fountain with underwater light and purple chrysanthemum might please for a while until the urge to alter the fountain starts. The next fountain might be of black slate with green ivy and a Buddha or copper oil lamp. Or a conch shell overflowing water to a scallop shell below, with air plants nestled in surrounding driftwood. What do the accents mean or tell you about your mood or your inner images? Check out the Symbols Dictionary. How do you nourish your human spirit? What pulls you forward toward your inner goals?

Readers Respond

North Carolina in the snow

"I first saw your demo on Interior Motives," writes Page Prewitt in North Carolina. "I bought the pump, etc. and made my first fountain the day I saw the show. I had to dig up rocks from under the snow. I have since made five fountains. I was in England last week and showed friends there how to make one. That fountain went home with another friend from Scotland. Several other folks there have since made fountains for themselves.

Curved water stairs, Fontaine des Innocents, Paris.

I made one for the living area of my house, for the master bedroom, for a sick friend, and one for my son's medical office. I love my fountains and they are wonderful fun to make!"
– Page Prewitt, North Carolina

The Fountain as Altar Piece

An altar is a raised place serving the purpose of sacrifice and other sacred acts in almost all religions. The elevated location represents raising gifts to a higher power. Some consider the altar the spiritual center of the world, a place of protection and refuge. Home altars are little tableaus, scenes to remind you of the sacred, where heaven and earth meet. The power of the builder and the power of the inspirational objects creates a communion of sacred energies.

Running water pours from vase cradled in woman's lap; garden setting. Photo © Nova Development.

Home altars are showing up across the country. As interest in Celtic mysticism, Neo-Paganism, and Native American spirituality spreads, more and more people are creating sacred spaces at home where they can reaffirm their spiritual strength, meditate, or enhance their relationship with the Divine.[19]

Altars tap into an ancient tradition learned from ancestors. Home altars are created in various forms, from small and simple to elaborate and multi-tiered, adorned with sacred or inspirational objects – rocks, statues, candles, photographs, ivory frogs, wooden figures.

Visualize your sacred space to decide what you need in it. Think about what is important or meaningful to you at this time in your life, suggests Peg Streep, author of *Altars Made Easy*.[20] Find a few inspirational things that you love and that inspire you; then get an attractive cloth and arrange the items in a way that feels right. Spend some time at the altar to see what feelings or insights come up.

Perhaps what's important to you at this time in your life is an image of flowing creativity.

A table top fountain is one option for an altar centerpiece. As a centerpiece, and having it's own sacred meaning (see Dictionary of Symbols), the fountain becomes a place of creative incubation. "If you have a sacred place, and use it," says Joseph Campbell, "something eventually happens."

Japanese garden lantern, a peaceful focal point in a table top fountain.

Villa d'Este, Campania, Italy.

Maybe you're not ready for an altar or may feel kind of shy or silly about creating one. Given the growing popularity of small fountains, putting a fountain garden together is one way to feel out the idea of altar building without embarrassment. Personal fountains seem to stimulate and release the inner creative wellsprings. What setting might you create to relax so creative juices flow?

Readers Respond

Nice to come home to

A fountain enthusiast writes, "I finished my first fountain and placed it in my 'spiritual corner' of my home. I am so pleased with the results. The fountain truly brings the outside indoors. I just love the way it sounds and looks. I used rocks from Japan, slate, aggregate, petrified glass, driftwood, ivy and a very simple glass bowl! Oh, and a tea light, too! Wow! It is so peaceful and beautiful and so nice to come home to. I now want to make a fountain for my workstation and one for my bedroom."
– Laura Cunningham, San Francisco, CA

The Meanings of Spring and Fountain

Water jets at the Louvre, Paris.

One way to ease into seeing fountains' possibilities is to understand the meaning of spring and fountain, especially spring, of which indoor fountains are man-made copies.

Spring as Running Water

A spring is a flow of water from the ground, often the source of a stream or pond.

Springs are associated with flow, current, course, tide race, rivulet, brook, and tributary.

Springs and fountains are images of the soul and life force; they represent hidden sources, spiritual energy, and individuality.

Inquiry: When are you in the flow? What obstructs your course?

Spring as Reserves
Fountains and springs are associated with unending supply.

A spring is treasure, stores, accumulation, reserve funds, and unlimited provisions.

Inquiry: How are your reserves of time, money, space, and energy? What drains your reserves?

Spring as Cause
A spring is the genesis, reservoir, fountain, or wellspring; it is the source, origin, or motive (as the "Fount of Abundance, Virtue, and Intellectual Life").

To spring is to appear suddenly as when curses spring from lips.

Spring refers to descent, derivation, remote cause, or influence (Achilles sprang from a line of kings).

Inquiry: What do you generate? Is it what you want? What springs from you?

Spring as Morning
Spring is that season of the year in which plants begin to grow after lying dormant all winter (a plant springs from a seed). In the North Temperate Zone, spring is generally regarded as including the months of March, April, and May, that period between the vernal equinox and the summer solstice.

Spring refers to any period of beginning or newness.

Inquiry: What is beginning to grow in you? How do you know?

Spring as Elasticity
A spring is a device, as a coil of wire, that returns to its original form after being forced out of shape.

Stone fountain. Mari, C. 2125-2025 BC. Water was piped in through a hole in the base and flowed from the vase held by the goddess. The flowing vase, as symbol of the source of all water and life, appears consistently West Asian art (After Moynahan, p.6).

Springing a leak: Hapless boat at the Villa d'Este.

Springs, resilient and elastic, absorb shock (bed-springs); springs are the motive power in clocks.

Spring is associated with resilience, buoyancy, recoil, bounce, rebound, and reflex.

Inquiry: How well do you bounce back? What is your optimal form?

Spring as Leap
A spring is a sudden and rapid movement upward or forward from the ground, by suddenly contracting the muscles (spring to one's feet).

Spring is associated with jump, romp, gambol, prance, and frolic; a Scottish dance.

To spring is to leap or come forth suddenly or to rise up above surrounding objects (tower steeple springing high above the town).

Inquiry: What makes you leap with excitement? What makes you spring into action?

Spring as Strength
Spring is power, energy, and force.

A spring in one's step means walking with elasticity, vigor, or spring.

Inquiry: What gives you vigor and energy? What is the source of your spring?

Spring as Surprise
"I'll spring for dinner" or "I'll spring him from jail" means I'll treat or bear the cost for someone else.

Another leaky boat, La Barcaccia, at the Piazza de Spagna, Rome .

One can spring a surprise, spring a trap (close or snap shut), or spring a military mine (explode it).

A boat can spring a leak, or suddenly begin to take on water.

Inquiry: How do you respond to the unexpected? What surprises you?

Spring as Architectural Feature

To spring is to rise from the impost with an outward curve.

The spring is the line or plane in which an arch or vault rises from its impost.

> Inquiry: How solid are your supporting structures? How firm is your foundation? What are you arching toward?

Spring as Warped, Split, Bent

To spring is also to bend or stretch a coil beyond the point where it will spring back fully.

A sprung door is loose, warped, or split.

To spring a mast or spar is to strain, break, or split by force.

A warped boat may spring a leak.

> Inquiry: Where are you split, bent, or strained? What needs to be done?

A spring-shaped playful snake from Stravinsky's kinetic (moving) fountain gallery, Paris. Note the black device below that rotates the snake.

A golden Buddha laughs at seeing a hidden spring; with coins, swedish ivy cuttings. Student composition, San Francisco Learning Annex, 2/98. Photo © Paris Mannion.

Sweet tempered ceramic figurine, patterned after stone Mari figure from 2000 B.C., demurely clasps an eternally gushing vase to her chest.

Chapter 3:
The Fountain as
an Act and Symbol
of Creation

How Do We Create and Why?

There are a variety of creation myths; many refer to the creation of consciousness, or how man became aware of himself as a thinking and feeling creature. These days people are coming into a new awareness of themselves as thinking and feeling creatures. We often overburden ourselves with the business of daily demands, sacrificing sleep and losing touch with a sense of well-being. But now many are turning to indoor fountains as a way to slow down, reevaluate priorities and establish a more natural balance. Some like the novelty of hearing water in unexpected places and the visual treat that awaits as they reconnect with nature. Others make fountains for their ease of construction and avenue for creative play. What about fountains attracts you? What will you create in your fountain garden?

The birth of Venus from the mussel. After Botticelli.

There are ten themes, described by Marie Louise von Franz, that account for creation.[21] Perhaps you might identify one of the ways you create in the process of building your fountain garden.

One theme shows how creation is an awakening toward consciousness. That is, the awakening toward consciousness is identical with the creation of the world. Many are awakening to the realization that life is out of balance; this realization is like coming out of an unconscious state. Creating a fountain garden is a tribute to and reminder of this new awareness.

For some building an indoor fountain is a conscious decision to make room for the natural world of bubbling springs and foliage. The garden surrounding a fountain symbolizes constancy and truth under difficult circumstances, as well as access to hidden springs and sources. What is it to be fluid and flexible?

For others, the desire for the sound of water fuels the action. Sound in some creation myths is a basic element, often the source or "voice" of the manifest world, the trigger by which the world comes into being. What motivates you? What are you building?

Another motif is the birth of the cosmos through groping about and accidental action; these movements are part of the unconscious creative process. After assembling materials to make a shell fountain where water drops at two or three levels, we often fumble about balancing or dropping things, watching something else slide into place or collapse. Creation appears to occur accidentally, and we keep at it, knowing there is always a way to make it work if the materials are right for the design. If they are not, what is the back-up plan? What are options for other situations in life? What plan do you need to create?

The myth of creation is also represented as a movement from above to below; a Spiritual Being in the Beyond creates by coming down or throwing things down. A man related how he'd been hit with the idea to build a miniature mill scene complete with water wheel. It came down in a "waterfall" of inspiration. He described the intense delight he took in building just that scene with a submersible pump and his ingenuity.

Sky: Heaven fertilizes the Earth and brings forth man; after Thenaud, Traite de la Cabalé, 16th century.

This idea of everything having a replica or model image in the sky is found in many civilizations as well as in Platonic philosophy. You might have an image of your fountain garden which seems to come down from above and whose reality is and remains in the Beyond even after you build it. Does this happen in other areas? What effect does this have on your values?

Another theme is creation resulting from a movement from below to above, the emergence of the world from a hole in the earth or beneath the sea. In the creation myth from India, the divine primeval life substance prepares to put forth the universe; the cosmic waters grow a thousand-petaled lotus of pure gold, radiant as the sun. The Absolute moves into creation through the lotus, also called the Golden Moisture or Goddess Earth. Her movement initiates each cycle or life-rhythm of birth through death. Where are you in the cycle of life? What more could you be?

Lotus: Smelling the life-giving fragrance of the lotus blossom. Detail after a mural in the Grave of the Night near Thebes, 18th Dynasty, ca. 1400 B.C.

Later the gods and demons, contending for world domination, conclude a temporary truce to extract the Elixir of Immortality from the Universal Sea which rests on a tortoise. This extraction is known as the churning of the Milky Ocean. Has something been churning in you or have you been diving deep into yourself? This process might find expression in a fountain. Don't be afraid to put any objects in your fountain; see how they are, and you can always change it. As long as the water stays in the container, there is no way to do it wrong.

Using images from the myth, one might accent the fountain with a stained glass lotus fitted over the pump spout, or with a lotus shaped floating candle. A turtle, elephant, or Indian goddess might be added. In Asia and India, the turtle symbolizes material existence, natural evolution, and longevity. The elephant stands for power, wisdom, peace, and happiness. What gives you strength? How are you evolving? What world are you creating? Perhaps a fountain theme emerges as if from below one's awareness.

Tortoise: Detail from a picture of the creation of the world in which the primeval sea of milk is changed into butter through periodic turning of the world axis, which rests on a tortoise. After a Hindu painting.

The motif of the twin creators or two animals appears in many creation myths.

The motif describes the separation of individual consciousness from its unconscious background; yet they belong together. The two animals or twins together represent the preconscious totality in which everything, including consciousness, is already contained.

Animals are frequent images of the animal aspect of the Self, symbolizing our instinctive nature and its connection with our surroundings. You might place your power animal or spirit guide next to the flowing source of life, acknowledging the larger consciousness that arises from keeping an eye on both the background and foreground. How would you pull this all together in a fountain?

The theme of Deus Faber, the godhead who manufactures the world, is represented in the Biblical creation myth. Renewed interest in the story of Genesis suggests many are reconsidering this creation myth in terms of human character and struggle. What struggles are you encountering? How might you represent this motif in a fountain setting?

The creator as first victim or source from whose parts the world is fashioned is another motif. In Chinese philosophy the universe came into being when the primordial One split itself into the two complementary principles of yin and yang. Yin-Yang then manifested themselves through the five elements of wind, water, metal, earth, and fire. The role of human beings is to maintain the harmony or tao of yin-yang in human affairs through the regulation of ch'i. Perhaps you might represent harmony using the five elements. How else do you express harmony? In what ways are you the source?

We also see it is not possible to create something without destroying something else at the same time. Creation is a sort of destruction or deconstruction so that the parts can be reassembled in a "better" way. Every step forward towards building up more consciousness destroys a previous living balance. So there is a certain instinctive resistance to letting go of even self-destructive behavior because the psyche tends to establish a balance or harmony. A neurosis is clung to until a new attitude becomes dominant. How reluctant am I to let go of a fountain composition when it's time to clean the bowl because I like things just the way they are? Where else do I do this in life?

Monstrous sea creature devouring hapless victims. Image © Nova Development.

The subjective moods of the Creative Being, such as discomfort and uneasiness, may lead to creation. The motif of anxiety is a deep irrational fear of the unexpected or of something new or of the unknown, the void. This anxiety often arises when one is unoccupied or alone in stillness.[22] The reason for the fear is the coming up of the unconscious. If you can stand the tension and panic and visualize the unconscious, or let it speak in images and stand the first impact, then you can uncover the first irrational fear. What keeps your creative process inactive? What are you tolerating?

Building a fountain garden is one way to objectify a depression for the purpose of healing. "The secret final intention of a depression," von Franz says, "is to depress, to lower the level of consciousness so that the creative process can come into action again."[23] Play with your fountain; you cannot do it wrong and you can change it in any way. What are you moving through?

Crafting your fountain garden can give symbolic representation to your inner state. Your fountain may also give artistic expression to subjective moods of laughing, yielding and of love. What is your prevalent mood? Is it a habit?

A basic primordial motif might find expression in your fountain garden. Primordial motifs include World Birth by Creative Fire, Seeds of the World, or the World Egg from which everything springs. Fire's power to destroy is often interpreted as the means to rebirth at a higher level. Seeds represent new beginnings and the abundance of possibilities not

Ptah shaping the world egg.

Tiered fountain with plants and stars. Image © Nova Development.

yet developed. As the germ of life, the egg is a widely recognized fertility symbol in ancient spring celebrations in Druidic and Indian creation myths.

The egg, as the symbol of the totality of all creative forces, was present at the primal beginning, often floating upon the primal ocean. It gave forth from itself the entire world. To represent this process, one might accent a fountain with a marble or cloisonné egg on a pedestal next to the ocean-water. Does this motif of world egg floating on primal waters appeal? Is your creative process one where ideas burst forth? What keeps you going? What is it to be exceptional?

The final theme, as practiced in sixteenth century alchemy, is creation through meditation. To make the Philosopher's Stone was to reproduce or create the world on a subjective level. Alchemy is a reversed or inward creation, in a way a mirror opposite of the cosmological outer theories. For example, in alchemy the vessel or fountain represented the whole universe, then considered a closed and circulating system. The vessel was a symbol of the human psyche as whole; within the vessel all the processes seen in the outer world can be conceived and experienced. Will your fountain be a miniature world? How are you the vessel?

The Fountain as Artistic Expression

When the fifteenth and sixteenth century alchemists talked about changing base matter or first matter into gold, they were referring to the desire to change the most base into the highest in value. They hoped to destroy in order to extract the panacea wherever it is hidden. "The adept's preoccupation with matter," says Jung, "can be seen as a serious effort to elicit the secrets of chemical transformation (but) at the same time . . .[was] the reflection of a parallel psychic process."[24]

Mercurius in the vessel with two rings of fire, after a 1718 illustration (Jung, CW 12, fig. 120).

Alchemists projected living qualities into their material because they considered both themselves and the matter on which they worked as part of living nature. Today we can recognize these projections as contents of the unconscious. In modern terms, we might define alchemy as the seemingly miraculous change of a thing into something better or more alive, through a method of transmutation.

Garden fountain supported by three figures, with background hills. Image © Nova Development.

The alchemists conducted the process of change partly in the library; there they studied ancient treatises on alchemy which gave esoteric directions for transforming matter. The other part was spent in the in the laboratory, washing, heating and distilling materials. This process was initiated and guided by the spirit of Mercurius, an evolved form of the Greek god Hermes.

Mercury

Mercury was to the alchemists a union of opposites–of dry and moist, of fire and water, of male and female. Mercury is the living water (or aqua vita), the fluid, elusive, changing and transforming substance. Mercury, in fact, is the only metal that dissolves gold and is liquid at ordinary temperatures. The spirit of Mercury is shown circulating through the Fountain of Life in Figure 22. In the psychological sense, Mercury is the symbol of the unconscious as well as of a union of the unconscious and the conscious. Can we be transformed by a fluid stream of awareness that a living fountain might stimulate? Is there some of "Mercury" in you? What has been eluding you?

Figure 22
The Fountain of Life as a Mercurial Fountain, Rosarium Philosophorum (1550), University of Glasgow.

The beginnings of a fountain garden project and attendant inner process might be

Alchemists at work: various stages of the process, after an illustration in Mutus Liber (1702) (Jung, CW 12, Fig. 133).

somewhat dark and obscure. In the Mercurial fountain (Fig. 22) serpents breathe poisonous fumes and vapors down around the fountain of life. The power of the Sun and Moon (later to be King and Queen) is obscured by the dark forces. Through washing and burning off impurities, the alchemist sought to transform the matter before him and reveal its true nature – gold – the panacea or immortal elixir.[25]

Maybe you've put off building a fountain for lack of time or maybe you couldn't find the right container or pump; or something else got in the way. The artistic expression of building one's indoor fountain is a reflection of the individuation process and can't be hurried. Are you ready to take action now? What else have you wanted to do and haven't? Where do you limit yourself?

Individuation means becoming aware of attitudes and behaviors that hold us back from a full life; then, through diligent effort, integrating the contents of the personal unconscious; and gradually achieving awareness of the self. Creating a fountain garden is another metaphor for the psychological process of individuation, a metaphor for the creation of gold from lead. How do I wash away impurities and defects to reveal my best self? Do I want to? Where am I resisting?

The Dragon

Consciousness is constantly threatened with being overwhelmed and 'swallowed up' by the archetypal images beyond awareness. Thus the process of individuation is often understood as an heroic venture or battle with the dragon, the unconscious, for the sake of achieving fully realized selfhood.[26]

Crowned dragon as tail-eater (1760).

In myths the hero is the one who conquers the dragon, not the one who is devoured by it, says Jung. And yet both have to deal with the same dragon, or dark corners of the personality. He who has faced the dark ground of his self and thereby gained himself "has arrived at an inner certainty which makes him capable of self-reliance, and attained what the alchemists called the unio mentalis [the one mind or united mind]."[27]

The dragon is a symbol combining the earth principle of the serpent and the aerial principle of the bird. In Fig. 23, Mercury is represented as a dragon. The dragon, Jung observes, is probably the oldest pictorial symbol. The dragon eating its tail represents eating up and assimilating the traits and behaviors that hold us back

Figure 23

Mercurius as Virgo standing on the gold (sol) and silver (luna) fountain, with the dragon as her son, after 16th century illustration (Jung, CW 12, Fig. 38).

from full self-expression. As the dragon dies, it arises again as the Philosopher's Stone or lapis. How do we withhold ourselves from life? What is it to be fully self-expressed?

Treasures guarded by dragons allude to the difficulties associated with struggle for wisdom. Dragons and crystals as fountain accents might bring to mind this struggle for greater self-awareness. The murmur of a fountain auspiciously placed, the negative ions clearing and lightening one's mood, can set the stage for looking at the truth about one's self – one's ego and a larger self. How can you figure out a suitable balance? Who are you becoming?

The accents in the fountain garden can link the fountain to an inner process of self-discovery and awareness. The artistic expression might stimulate questions such as, What am I creating? What is the meaning of my creation? or What is my focus? A fountain garden is one tool for the journey, an expression of an inner self as we unfold through time, with different fountain accents and themes catching our attention as an inner need arises.

Dragon: Michael battles the dragon. After an illustration in the Bamberg Apocalypse, *ca 1000.*

Sunken rectangular fountain with water jet in center and in foreground. Near Eastern Style.

Moving Water

The gushing up and flowing back of the Mercurial Fountain within its basin completes a circle, writes Jung. The circular sea with no outlet, which perpetually replenishes itself by means of a spring bubbling up in its center is an allegory of God. The sea is water's static condition; the "fountain" is its activation and the "process" is its transformation.[28] What would it be like to feel as if a spring were bubbling up in you? How do stasis and action alternate in your life? Does this image of the process fit you? What does? Can this be a playful image?

The enclosed garden, tower, cypress, and fountain are inviting feminine symbols (Figure 24). Yet the wall can symbolize hardships to be overcome before attaining a higher level of awareness. Is your "process" transforming you? How can you have it be easy in a trying period?

The fountain represents access to hidden springs and sources; water gushing forth symbolizes the life-force. In its circular basin, the fountain is an image of the soul as the source of inner life, spiritual energy, and individuality. What energizes you? What thrills you or inspires you?

The fountain as the upwelling of water is called by the alchemists the blessed or lustral water, wherein the birth of the new being is prepared. The fountain, the Water of Life, the source, also stands for the collective unconscious from which one hopes to differentiate oneself and become an individual. As you put the fountain together, you might ask, What values require my constant attention? or Who did I have to be to reach this place? In addition to conscious re-

Figure 24
The enclosed garden, fountain, tower and cypress are feminine symbols. Detail after a 17th c. devotional picture (Jung, CW 12, Fig. 26).

call, we may also get images from the unconscious.

A bonfire leaps in the night. Photo © Nova Development.

The Paradox of Opposites

The unconscious represents the autonomy of the psyche, reflecting in the play of its images, not the world but itself. Because it's not restrained by reason, the unconscious can accomplish the paradoxical union of opposites. In India the marriage of fire and water symbolizes their efficacy or power to produce intended results. The "union of irreconcilables" shown in Figure 25 represents the marriage of fire and water, a union of contrary qualities.

Fire is considered by many peoples to be sacred, purifying and renewing. Fire is the transmuting agent associated with strength, spiritual energy and animal passion. In alchemy the value of gold lay in its being a receptacle for fire, for the essence of gold is fire. It's opposite, water, is identified with intuitive wisdom, natural life, and possibilities.

In a fountain garden a candle flame makes a striking counterpoint to the cool water as an artistic expression of a symbolic union of opposites. As part of the individuation process, this "marriage" stands for a desire to unite in oneself the contrary qualities of fire and water. What are your passions? Your possibilities? What is your way?

Another way to represent the union of opposites is shown in Figure 26. Here a psychic pair of opposites can become creative of their own accord. One might experience this situation when, after a period of intense inner conflict, an unthought of solution (the child in the neck of the water-

Figure 25

The "union of irreconcilables": marriage of fire and water. The two figures each have four hands to symbolize their many different capacities (after an Indian painting) (Jung, CW 12, Fig. 72).

filled vessel) seems to emerge from the turmoil.

A child statue or photo, representing the unknown solution or creative impulse, might be placed in a fountain setting to stimulate new possibilities. What do you choose in any given moment? Where are you the solution?

Figure 26
Conjunction of opposites in
the Hermetic vessel or in the
water of the unconscious,
after 17th c. illustration
(Jung, CW 12, Fig. 226).

The Garden of the Philosophers

Another favorite symbol of the alchemists is the garden, also known as the sacred space. A walled garden suggests a mandala, center, or image of the self (Fig. 27). The garden is a symbol of earthly and heavenly paradise and of the cosmic order. In a garden nature is subdued, ordered and enclosed. Thus it is a symbol of consciousness, as opposed to the forest, the unconscious, where things grow wild. Does your fountain have a mandala design? Do you see the wild things as well as the ordered things? How do you decide to allow or include?

Shri-Yantra
Mandala.

In crafting a walled fountain garden one might use a jet or nozzle as shown in the margin, developed for Islamic fountains. What does your fountain garden look like in your mind's eye? Does it pull you in and offer rest and refreshment? What does? How can you pamper yourself today?

Your fountain can be a personal barometer: Is it well tended? Does it express your current mood? How can you change the fountain to reflect your inner state?

Bronze jet from
Moorish gardens
in Spain.

By putting together a fountain garden, with symbols you choose, you have the opportunity to establish a living connection with the Self. One may even become aware of an inner urge toward growth of the personality. "The inborn Self," says von Franz, "becomes more real within the receptive person than in those who neglect the Self. Such a person becomes a more complete human being."[29] While building the fountain, one might ask, "What is it to have a full, rich life?" and see how the process unfolds.

Figure 27
The Garden of the Philosophers:
the fountain in the walled
garden symbolized constancy
or perseverance in adversity –
a situation particularly char-
acteristic of alchemy. After an
illustration of 1702 (Jung,
CW 12, Fig. 84).

The alchemist ended his prayer for a successful outcome to the endeavor by saying "Deo concedente" or God willing. So let us say the same as we begin our laboratory work.

Fire and water unify this fountain of overflowing nautilus shell, coral, flowers and candles. The ceramic hors d'oeuvres dish from Good Will has built-in candle holders. Photo © Paris Mannion.

A miniature environment created with readily available materials: a fish "spitter" from a home improvement store; airplant; sandstone; and smooth, multi-colored pebbles, a pleasant reminder of afternoons spent at the beach.

Chapter 4: Materials and Where to Find Them

Also see Appendix B: Fountain Parts and Accents

Materials You Will Need

A container at least 2" deep and 6" across up to 12" deep and 2' or more across made of ceramic, clay, seamless metal, glass, plastic or wood with a plastic insert. If you decide on a ceramic bowl, be sure it is glazed on the inside. Check it for "weeping" by leaving water in it for a few days on a surface that will not be damaged if it does leak. Place a mat under the ceramic bowl when in use.

A beautiful blue glass bowl, suitable for fountain experimentation.

If selecting a clay bowl, seal carefully with three to four light even coats of waterproof sealant, such as a concrete and masonry lacquer or Seal Krete Waterproofing Sealer from a hardware store. Allow one to three hours to dry between coats. As with the ceramic bowl, check carefully for weeping. You may have a suitable bowl at home. Thrift stores, garden and craft stores, flea markets, and pottery stores have a wide selection. The wider the bowl, the more area for accenting.

A small submersible pump with water regulator. There are many styles available today. Five of the most popular ones are the Hagen Aquapump 1, Cal-Pump P-80, Rio 200, Rena Flow 80, and United Pump, Inc's Techna pump. Pumps range in price from $16 to $35 and are sold in aquarium, hardware, pottery and garden stores.

Cal Pump P-80. Photo © Paris Mannion.

Cal-Pump P-80 is available from the manufacturer at 818-364-2888. The Cal-Pump international number in Belgium is 011-323-652-1112. The Hagen international number in England is 011-441-977-556-

Aquapump 1; Circulation pump for fountain, waterfalls, hydroponics and aquariums. Flow regulator bar above intake valve (dark knob).

622. Aquatics Direct is a good pump source in England at http://www.aquatics-direct.com.

Tubing up to 10 inches that fits inside or outside the pump's spout. Purchase the tubing when buying the pump, trying different diameter tubing on the spout for proper fit. Some tubing is narrow and flexible, allowing it to be snaked around rocks or placed horizontally for a desired effect. Some tubing is stiff and wider, more suited for elevation of water. The price of tubing varies in hardware stores and in aquarium stores.

Gather stones to complement your container. Large round cobble stones, slate in many colors, small flat black rocks and other selections are found in bins at outdoor lawn and garden shops. Hardware stores sell bags of white decorative rock and smooth river rock.

Maybe you have your favorite rocks or will collect your own on the beach or in the hills. Scrub rocks thoroughly to remove grit and dirt; a mild bleach and water bath will get white rocks really clean.

Use bottled water if the water in your area is hard. Soft tap water seems to be okay to use in your fountain because the mild chlorination helps keep your fountain clean. Distilled water is not necessary. Bottled drinking water is fine.

You might prefer to buy a low maintenance, easy to assemble kit. Fountain kits are available on the Internet and from artisans. Some kits come with bowl, pump and tubing. Others contain a fountainhead, pump, and tubing. Some kits supply the stones as well or are "ready-made" fountains to which you can add personal accents. They are all to get you started experimenting.

Where to Find Materials

Rena pump and underwater light set.

(Also see Appendix B: Fountain Parts and Accents) These stores carry interesting items to personalize and accent your fountain garden:

Aquarium and pet stores. Aquarium stores carry the small submersible pumps as well as flexible tubing. They also have lava, tufa, and sandstone rocks which have naturally formed holes to place over the pump spout. You will also find small pagodas, bridges, and benches as well as glass beads, colorful aquarium rocks, and water plants. Some stores carry perforated tubing to direct sprays in a horizontal position and "Y" shaped spout attachments to divert water into two streams; however, the device may be too big for an indoor fountain.

Water plant in bloom. Image © Nova Development.

Catalogs, mail order and on the internet. Table top fountains, wall-mounted fountains, bird baths with recirculating pumps, and stones drilled so water will spurt out can be purchased through mail-order catalogs. On the Internet, search using "indoor fountains," "table top fountains", "waterfall fountains" and similar phrases.

Fountainheads. One artisan partnership has limited quantities of the popular inset acrylic tray on which to place fountain accents. These lightweight trays rest in bowls designed with the pump's cord exiting the base of the bowl so you may show off the fountain's beauty from all sides.

Other bowls are in earth-tone colors with the look of marble or granite. Larger bowls are designed to use an optional underwater light (available separately). The kit also contains the Aquapump 1 and 8" of plastic tubing.

Fountain accessories include a fountain cushion, a crushed velvet pillow on which the fountain is placed. The pillows come in a variety of colors to complement your fountain accents. The owners will also design a fountain for you. Ask about their "fountain in a basket" or attend Susan's fountain-flowing classes held in San Francisco and build your own.

To build your "dish of memories" with a variety of fountain supplies, call Susan Picklesimer or Diane Zack at Fountainheads (1-415-921-7902).

Lion spitter from Moses fountain, Rome.

Garden stores. These shops carry fasteners to hold flower stems, plants (such as ivy, spider and philodendron), bonsai trees, air plants such as tillisandria, and little orchids glued to small stones. From a feng shui perspective, silk or live flowers and plants are preferable to dried flowers and stems, but do what pleases you.

Garden stores also carry table top fountains, wall-mounted fountains, and other fountain accents such as affection stones inscribed with "serenity", "harmony", "peace", etc.

Lapidary and gem stores. These carry crystals, shells, stone slab clock faces (with a center hole, to create a waterfall), cloisonné eggs and egg stands, lapis, rose quartz and other decorative rocks, coral and sea sponges, sand dollars, sea urchins, and starfish, among other items.

Arrowhead sand dollar has a naturally formed hole to fit over a pump spout.

Michael's and other craft and hobby stores. These stores carry small wood and feather birds, feathers of many colors, silk flowers, bowls, bells, mirrors, and beeswax candles, as well as craft supplies like glue guns, Spanish moss, and spray paint. A waterproof adhesive, E 6000, for gluing rocks together, is also available at Michael's.

New Age and independent bookstores. Some carry beautiful copper oil lamps that cast a unique glow. Fueled by olive oil, the lamp's wick is a tiny cotton ball. For catalog, call Elezar (1-800-550-LAMP). Floating candles (including lotus shaped ones), crystals and stones, incense holders, books on gems, and assorted bells and chimes can often be found there.

Water spurts out of a giant metal "sea urchin". Jack London Square, Oakland, California.

Pier One, Cost Plus or other import chains. Look for glass beads and marbles, tea candle holders, incense containers, glass bowls, figurines, small brass framed mirrors, baskets of shells and many other items attractive in a fountain garden.

Fountain Pumps, Inc. This business focuses on indoor and outdoor fountain and pond supplies to the retail market. Offered are striking underwater lights that illuminate shells and crystals from below. The lights come in four colors (red, blue, green, yellow) and clear. For wholesale orders of pumps and lights, call Glenn Harrison at Fountain Pumps, Inc (800-207-3479).

Thrift stores. Good Will, Salvation Army, St. Vincent stores and others carry unusual containers that make wonderful fountain bowls. Glass punch bowls, wood salad bowls (when water sealed), and hors d'oeuvres platters can be recycled as indoor fountains.

Pan plays his flute.

Ross clothing stores have a homewares section with many beautiful and inexpensive bowls. And, of course, flea markets and garage sales yield their treasures.

Readers Respond

Woodland Magic

A happy fountain maker writes, "I made a beautiful fountain this weekend after a treasure hunt through Michael's, Ross, Home Depot, Target and a nearby nursery. It's a very woodsy fountain with a touch of magic – lots of plants, stones and moss as well as iridescent pebbles to compliment the abalone shell, floating candles and little mirrors to reflect the flowing water and glistening 'jewels'. A troll made of bark, pine twigs and acorns sits above. I created a backdrop with a large fern, little tropical palms and Pothos plant. I set a soft light lamp above to highlight it all.

Metal candle stand from import chain.

When stepping from the patio to indoors, you actually have the sensation of going OUTSIDE. I had to ask my husband 'Do you mind living in the woods?"
– Shelagh Kulchin, Woodland Hills, CA

Fountain Business

"I saw you on Interior Motives shortly after I had begun making fountains. I was so thrilled to see how you did your fountains and I immediately

A belled buoy alerts sailors to danger. Image © Nova Development.

ordered your book... I've begin to sell fountains quite successfully to stores here in Chicagoland and am continuing to grow and change in my designs. ... I have quite a demand for fountains with a southwestern theme.... Thanks..."
– Anita Fontana, Chicago, IL

Christmas gifts

"After getting your book I embarked on five fountains of my own. Four were Christmas gifts and they were a major hit! ... I am already getting hints from family and friends they want fountains for next year."
– Denise Wolff, Elburn, IL

This whimsical scene invites us to call a plumber, as water cascading out of a copper tee threatens to flood a nearby birdhouse. Student composition, San Francisco Learning Annex. Photo © Paris Mannion.

"Explore the wide variety of sounds and scenes a fountain can hold." Bamboo section fits atop the water spout in this fountain basket. Robert Birnbach, photographer. Susan Picklesimer, artist (415-921-7902).

To the right of the tall orange flower, water flows into one shell and then another as a green frog looks on. The tan stone at right is etched with "serenity". Student composition, Palo Alto Adult Education, 3/98. Photo © Paris Mannion.

A fountain owner adjusts the placement of an airplant.

Chapter 5: Assembling your Fountain

General Instructions

You now have a container, submersible pump, tubing (if desired), stones, and a small plant or cuttings and are ready to assemble your fountain. Examine the pump and set the spout in place. For our example we use the Hagen Aquapump 1.

Following the directions included with the pump, ease off the front and back panels from the pump, wiggling the panel back and forth as you pull. Then you can attach the rubber suction cups which hold the pump in place. With the front panel off, note the propeller blades; gently lift the propeller out, and you will see the ceramic shaft. Drop the magnetic shaft back in its compartment and proceed.

Slide in the "feet" or little suction cups to the base of the pump and set the regulator on "low". Wet the bottom of the container; and place the pump in the center or rear of the container, pressing down slightly to achieve suction. This eliminates vibrational sounds when the pump is running. The pump can be rearranged by sliding it around. Remember, the pump cannot run dry or it will be permanently damaged.

Have towels nearby to mop up if splashing gets out of hand. Add enough water to cover the intake valve, about 1 1/2 inches. Cut a length of tubing if desired and fit onto the spout. Making sure the plug is dry, plug the pump into your outlet As illustrated, you can create a dew loop in the cord to eliminate any chance of water reaching the outlet.

Dew loop.

*Symmetrical oval
container allows
water to spill over
into basin below.
Near St. Peter's,
Rome, Italy.*

How is the water volume? Adjust the regulator if needed and add more water. The smaller and shallower the bowl, the more often you will need to replenish evaporated water.

Begin building your fountain at the rear of the container by adding stones behind the pump and where the cord exits. This will camouflage the cord. Mount the stones, larger ones on the bottom, to create a high to low effect or design it however you please. Larger stones around the pump's intake valve will ensure that water flow is unrestricted. The water will make pleasant soothing sounds as it flows to its lowest level. Experiment combining dark and light stones. If recessing a tea candle among the stones, make a hollow in which to set the candle where water won't extinguish the flame.

If using a deeper bowl or large colorful "fish bowl" flower pot, you'll need plastic tubing up to 10" long, depending on how high you want the water to rise. The right tubing will fit snugly over the removable nozzle of the pump. Filling the bowl with 5 or 6 landscaping or cobble stones may be more convenient than using many smaller stones. Or chunks of lightweight, porous lava rock may be used to fill up the bowl. Lava rock absorbs water, so check the water level as you build. Smaller stones may be slipped into crevices later and will soften the water sound. Adding more water will also soften the sound in deep bowls.

*Colorful "fish
bowl" container
with water flowing
down amethyst
chunk. Photo ©
Paris Mannion.*

Continue adding your personal touches, plugging the pump in now and then to see how and where the water is flowing. Rocks that are hit by water and also touch the edge of the bowl will conduct water out of the bowl and contribute to the splash factor. Expect that there will be some splash as you get things organized. A meat baster can suction out excess water displaced by stones.

Plug in the pump again. If the pump gurgles, spews or "burps", try partially covering the spout to restrict the water flow and remove air bubbles. Be sure the pump has enough water to function. Or add a heavier stone to the top of the pump behind the spout to be sure the suction cups remain secure. Plastic tubing of even 1/2" will quiet the pump.

A small capstone or concave stone or shell can be angled across the pump spout to redirect or diffuse the water flow. Slate pieces of varied colors can be angled to form a pyramid, with water bubbling out the top. Or water can be directed into a conch or scallop shell and then overflow into a shell on a lower level.

The more water you design your fountain to hold, the more efficiently the pump will operate and the less often you will have to replenish the water. The pump should work noiselessly and the water flow smoothly.

Water jets from the rim toward the center as well as out of the fish's mouth as the riding boy looks on. Image © Nova Development.

Four ways to regulate the water sound:

• Raise or lower the water level (siphon with a meat baster)

• Raise or lower the water pressure on the pump's regulator

• Put something under the water flow to catch it or divert it in its travels

• Partially obstruct or divert the water outlet by leaning a curved shell or stone over it

What are your techniques?

Five ways to turn your pump off and on

(without getting under the couch to find the outlet)

Spiky air plants contrast with the smooth bowl of this small fountain. Photo © Paris Mannion.

Unique "ice cube" fountain with lustre gems in a glass baking dish. Photo © Paris Mannion.

• Plug the pump into a wall switch and turn it on from the wall.

• Plug the pump into a timer so it will go off and on automatically.

• Use a remote control to start or stop the pump.

• Plug the pump into an extension cord that has a switch.

• Use a low voltage pump with transformer and off-on switch such as the Rena pump.

More building techniques.

Another fountain style is the inverted clay pot. Put the pump in your fountain bowl and place the pot over the pump's tubing so it rises out of the clay pot's drainage hole. Place stones and fountain accents around the clay pot. The clay pot approach means a lighter weight fountain with fewer stones.

A variation on this style is the wire basket turned upside down and adjusted over the pump spout. Or a stiff wire mesh net can be laid across the bowl, braced by the bowl's inner edge. Cut a hole in the wire mesh for the pump spout or tubing. Then arrange rocks and your favorite fountain accents on top of the wire basket or mesh.

"Lion's Paw" fountain features air plant, water rippling over a shell's edge. Photo © Paris Mannion.

Or use a plastic plate or plexiglass that fits inside a round fountain bowl. Drill or carve a hole to the side or in the center for the pump tubing. Water will come up, spread across the tray, and drop back into the bowl. Build up your fountain scene on top of the tray. Luster gems show up nicely in this arrangement.

Another technique to minimize fountain weight is to fill the container with chunks of styrofoam. Then place fountain accents and favorites stones on top to cover the styrofoam.

My thanks to the savvy folks at ttfountains@onelist.com for some of these styles.

If using a fountain kit, assemble according to instructions. (See Materials, Part A) You are now ready to personalize your fountain with accents of your choice.

A bird on driftwood looks over a fountain (broken pottery neck) with multicolored pebbles, moss. Photo © Paris Mannion.

Assembling a Fountain

Step 1:
Place plastic tube on pump, set waterflow to low or medium, and put pump in bowl.

Step 2:
Add water to cover pump's intake valve. Press pump down so suction cup feet grip securely. Plug the cord into electric outlet.

Step 3:
Add rocks around pump and back of bowl.

Step 4:
Begin accenting with favorite rocks as you build up the design.

Step 5:
Add plants, flowers, or other favorite accents.

Step 6:
Our finished fountain.

Step 7:
A closeup view.

Step 8:
A closeup of the stone frog.

Assembling an Abalone Fountain

Step 1 :
Start out as you did in the general assembly instructions: add tubing to your pump, place it in the container, and add water. Add rocks to the bottom of your container and a platform for the abalone like the sandstone pictured here.

Step 2:
Place the abalone shell where the water will come out of the holes yet stay in the bowl.

Step 3:
See how it flows. Adjust the abalone. If the shell is based on a flat, unpolished rock, it will hold its balance better. Wedge little stones under different parts of the shell to keep it stable.

Step 4:
Camouflage the back of the plastic tube by leaning a decorative rock against it or nestle some silk flowers by the plastic tube.

Photos © Paris Mannion

Some Abalone Variations

Variation 1 (two views):
Two or more abalone shells are used, with water cascading from one shell to another.

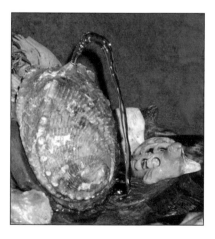

Variation 2:
Tubing from the pump is wedged in one of the shell's holes, so that water spurts out.

Making & Assembling a Blue Mountain Fountain

This project is made out of clay in a ceramics class. Ceramics classes are offered in Recreation Centers and Adult Education schedules. These are nice because one can work at home preparing, shaping, and drying the pieces, then bring them into class for glazing and firing.

Step 1:

The mountain is a hollowed out mound of clay, hopefully a uniform 1/2" thick. The clay gets thin inside because of scraping away outside clay to form channels or switchbacks for the water to flow down. Pad the inside with clay to build it back up to 1/2". Uniform thickness will promote more even drying and fewer cracks during firing.

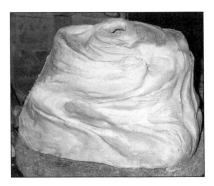

Step 2:

An oval clay bowl was shaped in class with a curved divider strip to separate water in the background from the dry foreground. The sides need to be at about 3" tall to accommodate shrinking when the clay dries. The pump needs about 2" of water to function optimally.

Tutorial photos © Paris Mannion; "palm tree" photo © Tanya Inman

Step 3:
Ready for the mountain. The foreground has been filled with soil and plants. The water basin has been prepared with the pump and tubing the same height as the mountain that will sit over them.

Step 4:
The Blue Mountain Fountain. Here the foreground has been arranged as a sitting place near a mountain stream and pond. The foreground could be filled with sand, all plants, animal figurines, or just about anything you imagine.

At left, we've tried a miniature "palm tree", actually an inexpensive look-alike fern from a home improvement store.

You could make a Red or Yellow Mountain Fountain depending on the color glaze you choose. Happy experimenting!

Build a Grotto!

Dark and mysterious, these caves near water cast a particular spell. Some caves were made into Christian shrines; Lourdes, for example, is a religious cave. Other caves were cult sites in prehistory, showing traces of the Ice Age. Caves are often the meeting places of deities and fore bearers and are associated with the realm of death (the dark realm) and of birth (the womb).

Renaissance Italian gardens and fountains used the grotto as illusion and entertainment, sometimes spraying unaware visitors with water jets. Before their removal to the Academia museum in Florence, Italy, Michaelangelo's unfinished slaves decorated a Florentine grotto, made for the tomb of Julius II.

Neptune behind a wall o'water, Villa d'Este, Campania, Italy.

Horse in Grotto, Piazza Navona, Rome.

Grottoes' romantic potential ensured that water caves would be incorporated into European gardens throughout the 17th and 18th centuries. In Germany, highly ornate grottoes were made at Wilhelmshöhe near Kasel and at Rococo gardens such as Vietschochleim in Bavaria.

Step 1:

To make an indoor fountain grotto plan for a bowl about 8 - 10" wide. Set the pump in the bowl, regulator on medium or high, and place about 3 - 5" of tubing on the pump depending on how tall you want the cave to be. Face the tubing's curve toward the bowl's center so it will direct water flow forward. Place flat stones on either side of the pump to build up the cave's exterior. Here we used sandstone, that versatile fountain filler.

Tutorial photos © Paris Mannion; grotto photos © Tanya Inman

Step 2:
We leaned a long, narrow piece of sandstone against the tubing, effectively hiding it. Fill the bowl with water to cover the pump intake valve and plug the pump in.

Step 3:
Continue layering stones on either side of the pump until you have the desired elevation.

Step 4:
Put a flat rock between the two stacks, connecting them; does the pump spout rest on the cross piece? If not, either cut the tubing or layer up more side rocks until it does.

Does the water fall to the sides but not over the edge? Try tilting the cross piece down a little. Is water pressure too low to create a fall? Adjust the pump to increase pressure. The water probably won't fall in a sheet, but you will get steady rivulets coming down over the mouth of the grotto.

Step 5:
Add stones to cover the back of the pump and tubing, and to enclose the cave. Place a few flat stones on top of the pump spout to hide it. Decorate the side steps with luster gems, crystals, or air plant. Slip spider plant cuttings or a floating candle in the water. Here we've placed our favorite Buddha, arms upheld with gold found in this treasure cave.

Make a Mask Fountain!

Wall fountains as masks with a water spout are all over Italy. The mask is an ancient form of an expressive facial disguise. Masks served to frighten enemies and played a part in magical rites.

Masks depict spirits and the personified powers of people or of animals. Simply as a face, the mask expresses the solar and energetic aspects of the life-process. The mask of Mithras, for instance, represents the Persian image of the Sun. Fountain masks or faces are a favorite theme in Rome. Water spouting from satyr-like faces is based on the ancient belief that every stream has its presiding deity.

Mithras.

The mask is also a kind of chrysalis, behind which something is transformed. The metamorphosis must be hidden from view.

The Bocca della Verita, or Mouth of Truth, may have been a drain cover dating from before the 4th century BC. Its formidable jaws would snap shut on the hands of liars, said medieval tradition.

Bocca della Verita. A huge masked fountain stands in the courtyard of the 5th century basilica Santa Sabina in Rome. It guards the gateway to the Park of the Orange Trees associated with the Knights of Malta.

Fountain masks for your water garden can be of various materials: ceramic, glass, water sealed wood, metal, and stone for instance.

Santa Sabina.

Tutorial photos © Paris Mannion; mask photos © Tanya Inman

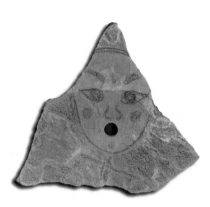

Step 1:

Choose a bowl about 10-12" in diameter. Several factors will influence the bowl diameter:

- how tall your mask is
- how you angle the mask on the supporting rocks
- how high you set the pump's water volume regulator
- how far out you want the water to shoot

We've taken a piece of drilled sandstone and drawn a face on it. The mask is drawn in colored pencils, which give a pastel image that blends with the pale shades of surrounding rocks.

Try non-water soluble paint to accent the mask with bright colors. Follow the manufacturer's painting instructions.

Step 2:

Place the pump in the bowl and set the water regulator on medium. Put a 1" long piece of 5/8" tubing over the pump spout. Step down the tubing diameter with a 3" length of the more flexible 3/8" tubing. This will give a horizontal bend to the water flow. Then, step up the tubing diameter again with another 1" long piece to fit through the mask. If you only have one diameter of tubing, that will do all right as there are adjustments you can make.

Layer flat rocks like sandstone in the bowl in front of the pump. Hold your mask vertically on the top layer.

Step 3:

Is the mask too tall for the pump spout? You can replace the middle tubing to lengthen the water reach. Is it too short for the pump spout? Prop up the mask with another layer of sandstone.

Do you want the mask positioned straight up and down? Hold it in place and wiggle the plastic tubing through the hole. If you have just one piece of less flexible 5/8" tubing, you may need to adjust the slant of the mask so the base is a little forward. The upper part of the tubing will catch and hold in the hole. Wedge stones around the mask on the ledge to stabilize it.

Fill bowl with water to cover the pump intake valve and plug it in. Try angling the mask for different effects.

Step 4:

How does the water fall? Control the sound and splash by using a sound stone that the water hits directly. This sound stone will diffuse water and minimize splash.

To disguise the pump spout in back, build up behind the mask with rocks that stay put. Here we've used round rough sandstone.

Step 5:

Continue accenting with plant cuttings, candle, luster gems, whatever compliments your mask, face, or mood. Voilá, a new mask fountain!

Photos © Paris Mannion

Using a "Spitter"

Step 1:
These are really for larger out-door fountains. To use in a table top fountain, look for a "spitter" which has fairly close water entrance and exit points. This fish has the water entrance point underneath, near the front. The advantage is that the pump can be near the side of the bowl that the fish rests on. The water jet will stay in the bowl.

However, some turtle and frog spitters have the water entrance point at the end of the animal, far away from the spitting mouth. In this case you'll need thinner plastic tubing (3/8" or less) to curve up from the pump spout. The tubing goes around to the outside edge of the bowl where it will fit the spitter resting on the bowl's edge.

Step 2:
Adjust the water flow regulator to control the arch of the spitting water. Begin adding stones to fill in the design. The design need not be pre-planned. Sometimes spontaneity is best.

Step 3:
Here we placed a piece of slate for the water to hit so it runs back down into the bowl. Water glistens as it flows down the dark stone, adding another point of interest. Finish accenting with air plants, ivy sprigs, shells, a candle or whatever you like.

Make a Spiral Watercourse!

Since prehistoric times, curves, scrolls and s's are an essential motif in ornamental art the world over. Spiral cave art appears in Europe and marine cultures like Crete and Egypt, and in ground level water channels in the Middle East, to name a few places.

Scholars debate the symbolic content of spirals which can include

Spiral ceiling art from Egypt, 7th c. BC (E. Wilson, 1986, Fig. 59).

- growth, renewal and return

- lunar cycles

- cosmic forms in motion

- unity and multiplicity

- evolution of the universe

- rotation of the earth

- relation between the circle and the center, and

- dancing, healing and incantations

The double spiral, closely linked to water, represents transition, regeneration and completion. The spirals in this fountain example curve to the left before interlocking. The left curve is an attribute of the whirlwind of Poseidon, lord of earthquakes and the sea. The right curve in a clockwise direction is an attribute of Athena, goddess of wisdom and of war.

These linking water spirals were inspired by the interlocking design in a Muslim water channel. Building things from scratch is a practical way to experiment with new ideas and prototypes.

Photos © Paris Mannion

Step 1:
The inside clay slab was 2.5" thick before drying. It measured 7" x 8" and dried for 2 weeks before the first firing. The hole on the slab for the pump spout is better too large than "just right" as there is more shrinkage here than in thin flat pieces. If cracks develop in the glazing process, they can be filled in with concrete and masonry sealant or epoxy putty. In this case, both remedies were applied.

Step 2:
The 8"x9" hand-built bowl was designed to give the slab about 1/2" clearance all around for water to flow off the slab and down the channel constructed for it. It was 3 1/2" tall (inside measurement) before drying. Small notches were cut on the corners for the cord to go over as it exits the bowl.

Step 3:
Set the pump on low or medium and place it in the corner. Fit and hold the water spiral fountainhead over the pump spout. Prop the slab up from underneath by filling the bowl with rocks. Fill with water and plug in. The water spiral can be tipped and adjusted somewhat to get a different path on the watercourse way or to alter the sound. Accent as desired with ivy cuttings, figurines, luster gems, favorite stones, an oil lamp.

Using Fountain Jewelry

Perhaps you have a favorite necklace you haven't worn for a while, or a bracelet handed down to you by a loved one. Displaying these pieces in your fountain will enhance its appearance and allow you to enjoy them every day.

Earrings:
Beaded amethyst earrings relax on stones, their ends trailing in the water. A verdi gris lizard looks on, enviously.

Bracelet:
The intense color and smooth texture of the bracelet contrasts with the rippled surface of the shells.

Necklace:
A necklace, forgotten by an absentminded mermaid, drapes across a nautilus shell. The glued-on clasp fastening the smooth rutilated quartz eventually came loose, so she looked for a pierced stone to sway in the water.

Photos © Paris Mannion

An old man holds a child on his lap beside a bubbling spring, wet rocks and spider plant. Student composition, San Francisco Learning Annex, 3/98. Photo © Paris Mannion.

A vine threaded through loops frames this unusual fountain; with ivy and sandstone. Student composition, Mountain View/Los Altos Adult Education, 4/98. Photo © Paris Mannion.

Etruscan lady waits patiently for her turn to grace a fountain.

Chapter 6:
Suggestions for Accenting Your Fountain

Aroma therapy. A small, two piece aroma therapy container can be placed on the rocks by the flowing water. Add a tea candle to the bottom part, water and essential oils to the top, and enjoy the fragrance! Or add a few drops of essential oil such as lemon or peppermint directly to the water. The effect is more subtle than in warm water. A few drops of essential oil once or twice a week doesn't seem to harm the pump or pets who drink from the fountain.

Hollow bamboo. Place the pump under water to the side or center of the bowl. Attach over the spout a flexible tubing about 3/8" to 5/8" diameter and 12" long. The other end of the tubing can be snaked around to a higher level and inserted into a length of hollow bamboo 6" to 8" long. The length depends on how far apart the growth rings are spaced and the size of your bowl. Place the hollow bamboo horizontally. and note where the water will pool. When the pump is turned on, the water is lifted out of the container, up the tubing, to flow down through the hollow bamboo back into the basin.

If not water sealed, bamboo pipes in constant use will turn black over time. This can be prevented by using Fountain Block, the first algae-removing product for fountains, available at pond supply stores. Eventually, however, the untreated wood will begin to shred. A marine varnish is one sealant but it is sticky and smelly.

Bark and petrified wood. The bark of pepper and birch trees has unusual color and shape and can be worked into driftwood creations. Keep dry.

Aroma therapy: healing scents from the goddess.

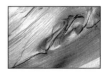

Bark & wood lend texture and contrast to the indoor fountain. Photo © Nova Development.

Bird's eye view of a birdbath.

Bird bath on a pedestal. Provided the basin is at least 2" deep, a birdbath can house a fountain garden. You might accent the fountain with tiers of overflowing shells. This elegant interior addition, with ferns or flowering plants arranged around the pedestal, can be placed in an area of filtered sunlight.

Birds. Birds carved from shell or wood, or small porcelain, feather or glass birds add an element of lightness and life. A feathered red bird, for instance, might perch on a piece of driftwood overlooking a bubbling spring.

Candles. Tea candles,votive candles in containers, or small candles on brass stands add an interesting contrast to flowing water. A copper oil lamp using olive oil for fuel and cotton for a wick is particularly attractive when set near the water. A stone oil lamp set among stones or a candle shaped and colored like a rock is particularly striking.

Copper plumbing tee.

Copper or brass fountainheads. Found in the plumping department of hardware stores, one and two inch long copper pipes fit comfortably over most pump spouts. The bright copper complements many shades of slate, sandstone, and sunburst cobble as water bubbles freely out of the center spout.

Another copper fountainhead is T-shaped so water comes out of two openings. A third copper piece is the "elbow" which curves, sending water out sending water out in an arch. These pieces can be polished if they start to tarnish.

Crystals. Crystal clusters, such as amethyst or clear quartz, add sparkling highlights. Rose quartz, turquoise, lapis, malachite, tiger's eye, or any colored stones you like will make the fountain garden distinctively yours. Peacock ore loses its color if submerged for a few hours. Any stone with iron in it will begin to rust, so keep these on dry land.

Amethyst candle holder.

Crystals of Light are amethyst and clear quartz clusters carved out to hold a votive or tea candle. The flame sparkles on the crystals and highlights the water. Call Natural Wonders (1-800-296-6337) for a store near you. Or order by mail from South Pacific Wholesale Co. (1-800-338-2162) in Vermont.

Eggs, the "germ of life". Colored marble eggs with a flower angled in between might be the accent in a kitchen fountain. Paperweight eggs of lapis, sodalite or malachite might be placed on an egg stand. The egg's round shape complements dark, round rocks and contrasts with irregular, angled rocks. Rose quartz eggs have their own special charm.

Lapis Lazuli egg on seahorse stand.

Feathers. Some time beach combing can yield a nice collection of white, tan, brown and gray feathers to feather your fountain nest if you wish. Craft shops, Indian specialty shops, and some pet stores carry an assortment of vividly colored feathers, symbol of air and wind. Feathers can be placed between rocks or glue-gunned to driftwood, shells, or stones to make a special accent.

Flowers. Silk flowers or live flowers make colorful additions to a fountain garden. Silk flowers can be tucked in between rocks, and cut flowers can float in the water or be anchored in metal fasteners. Live flowers left in the fountain water for more than three days or so may cause the water to become murky. The container and pump will need to be cleaned more often or use Fountain Block.

Blue glass vase for holding flowers.

Or put flower stems in a little vase and place the vase partially submerged in the water or between the rocks. Little orchids glue gunned to flat stones (nursery) make an unusual flower accent.

Glass, beads and stained. Beads with a flat bottom called "luster gems" come in eye-catching colors. They pick up the light in hues of blue, peach, red, green, clear, yellow. Selections vary at Michael's Arts & Crafts and Ben Franklin Crafts. Also look for glass marbles to fill glass fountain bowls.

A rose or gardenia blossom floating in your fountain perfumes the air. © Nova Development.

If you are handy with stained glass, you might make a flower-shaped flat piece with a small center hole to be laced over the pump spout. The

Antique incense burner. Image © Nova Development.

water flows up and over the glass, creating a waterfall. An underwater light or candle behind the waterfall will show off the stained glass.

Incense burners. Incense cones can be burned in a small dish, shell, or incense statue set on a fountain stone. Incense granules can be burned on top of charcoal in a saucer. Incense adds another dimension to the senses already stimulated by the flowing water and flickering fire.

Jewelry. Ankle and wrist bracelets and necklaces make attractive drapes over stones and pieces of wood. Pins and rings can be propped against rocks or partly submerged. A sapphire ring, an old piece of jewelry from another generation, sometimes adorns Kwan Yin when she graces a fountain. A hook earring or a stone necklace might dangle from an overflowing nautilus shell. Make sure the stone is not held in place by a clasp or pinchers or it may eventually fall off the the necklace.

Lava rock (pumice), sandstone, and tufa rock. These irregularly shaped rocks are about 4" to 8" in diameter and have one or two naturally formed holes. Set vertically in a fish tank, the fish swim through or hide in the lava tunnel.

Set horizontally over the pump spout, lava rock creates a distinctive water flow pattern, as if bubbling again out of a hidden spring or volcano. Lava is porous and absorbs water so you may not get the trickling sound you want at first. Water seal the rock with concrete and masonry lacquer so the water will slide off the rock, making a pleasant water sound. Fill in larger holes with pebbles to disguise the pump spout.

Beach stones with holes bored completely through by sea urchins and other creatures are a natural fountainhead.

Mirrors or picture frames. A small unframed mirror (about 2" square, oval, or octagon from craft stores) may be placed under the water flow

Stone beads.

to reflect the stream. A mirror behind a fountain will expand its energy. Or place the mirror behind a candle.

Picture frames of wood or metal in oval, square or round shapes lend color, texture and depth to a fountain garden. The frame can hold an image of a dear one.

Pebbles: Multicolored, white, black, or mixed, these may be used instead of larger rocks to fill in your fountain design. When wet the multicolored especially show their true hues. Low cost pebbles are found in big bins a outdoor garden centers.

A variety of multi-colored, semi-precious pebbles, contrasted with a shell cross section. Photo ©Nova Development.

Plants in small containers, water plants, plant cuttings, air plants, and bonsai trees. Keeping plants such as ferns, violets or miniature roses in their own containers prevents the soil from mingling with the fountain's water. The fountain water stays cleaner.

Water plants from aquarium stores can float on the water surface with no soil to hinder their suspended roots. Water hyacinths last about three months indoors near natural light. Like the bonsai, they are generally outdoor plants.

Bonsai tree.

Plant cuttings of ivy, spider plant, or pothos may be placed directly in the water whey they will develop roots. They may be planted in soil later and new cuttings added to the fountain. Depending on the size of your fountain, you'll need to refresh the water after about two weeks. Or a votive candle holder set among the rocks might be a vase for small plant cuttings.

Air plants, alone or glued on shell or wood, bring a pale green and flowery elegance to the fountain setting. A bonsai dish can be worked into a fountain's larger container to create a natural scene in miniature (Tip: read up on bonsai maintenance first).

Large red clay saucers. These 3" deep saucers, used under outdoor pots, serve as hand-

Airplant.

Pine: Ancient bronze pine cone from a fountain in the Vatican.

some fountain garden containers. Long, narrow slabs of red or metallic flagstone can be placed with the ends jutting or leaning out over the saucer's edge and the fountain built up in the center. The container's edge is then concealed, creating the image of a free-standing fountain. The upward angled flagstone also minimizes the splash factor. Water hitting the flat stones flows back into the basin. For best results, waterproof the saucer with several coats of sealant such as concrete and masonry lacquer.

Two red clay saucers. A variation on the theme above is to place a smaller saucer (perhaps 15" in diameter) inside a larger one (perhaps 18" in diameter), and build the fountain in the smaller saucer. Then fill the space between the two saucers with dirt and plant ivy or other low indoor vegetation, creating a garden surrounding the fountain. Water seal both containers first.

Seeds, nuts, and pods. Acorns, pine cones, star anise and other life-bearing kernels of nature give a distinctive texture and subtle scent to the fountain garden. Keep the accents out of water if not water sealed.

Shells, coral fans or clusters. Items from the sea add a pleasant touch; you may already have a few favorites. When placed right next to the water spout, a conch, scallop, oyster, or abalone shell will collect flowing water. The water then overflows the shell into the bowl. To create additional overflow, add another shell tier. Water can be directed to the top of a coral fan and flow down the branches, back lit by an underwater bulb.

A seashell of the spiky variety.

The vertical cross section of a nautilus shell, with its well marked spirals, makes a striking fountain centerpiece. Use about 2" of tubing on the pump, build up next to the tubing with flat or angled stones and brace the shell horizontally, spirals up, with modeling clay or rough pebbles. When the pump is turned on, water will flow over the ribbed spirals and down the rocks.

Or use a full nautilus shell. Add about 2" of plastic tubing to the pump spout, angling it so it points to and touches the rim of the nautilus shell. Build up under the shell and stabilize it. Keep water handy to add to the fountain in case the nautilus stores too much before it spills over. Adjust the shell angle.

Whole Nautilus shell.

Slate, flagstone, and other stones. Many varieties of flagstone and other decorative and landscaping rocks will add unusual sheen and color to your fountain garden. Go on a nature hunt or visit a garden center. A few favorite stones:

Apache Moss back: dark pink with small patches of dried green moss.

Apache Paint Flagstone: mottled pink, red and tan patches with a metallic sheen.

Arizona Million Dollar Buff: pale yellow and tan flagstone with a metallic sheen.

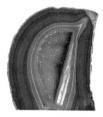

A bright blue geode, with sparkling crystal interior.

Sedona Red Flagstone: red clay-colored slabs about 1 - 2" thick.

Sunset Quartz: pale orange slabs with flecks of shiny quartz.

Quartzite: flat rock with a silvery-metallic sheen.

Sunburst Cobbles: advertised as "the color of the sky at sunrise and sunset", these 4" x 6" cobbles are a mix of pink, yellow, and orange patterns.

Mojave Mint: irregular chunks of light green rock.

Small statues and figurines. Any small object you like can be used to decorate or give significance to your fountain garden. Angels, fairies, totems, animals, fetishes, Buddha, Mary, or Kwan Yin and a few suggestions. Fairies, for

A smiling fountain shower bather, Photo © Paris Mannion.

Stone carved with a wave motif. © Nova Development.

Smooth rocks carved with contemplative mottos.

A brass bell.

instance, have a special significance. In ancient Mesopotamia fairies as the "soul" of landscapes took the form of the Lady of the Fountain and the Lady of the Water.

Carved stones, totem or affection. Totem animals are often carved into jasper and unakite. In one style the totem figure is carved into the stone and is then painted black or gold. Affection stones or "blessing stones" are smooth oval stones about 3 - 4" long, inscribed with wishes such as serenity, friendship, wisdom, and love.

Sliced stone with a center hole (used for clock faces in lapidary stores). These pieces with naturally patterned designs are about 1/4-1/2" thick and 4-6" in diameter. The drilled hole is smaller than the pump spout and water will jet out if the stone is set directly on the spout. Elevate the sliced stone about 1/3" above the spout by propping it up with 3 or more pebbles. A unique dimension is created when water rises through the center of the flat, sliced stone and cascades off the edges in a lovely waterfall.

Trees made of copper wire or driftwood. Sometimes small ready-made copper trees can be found at thrift stores. Or you can fashion your own with heavy copper wire. For a driftwood tree, use pieces of driftwood, a glue gun, and Spanish moss. Then you will have a symbolic Tree of Life next to your fountain's Water of Life.

Wind chimes or bells. Chimes and bells are a feng shui cure to lure in ch'i (and customers) because they produce noise. Place the wind chime stand on a flat rock. The small clusters of chimes or pendants of glass, ceramic, or metal hang so they strike one another and tinkle when blown by the wind. Or given a slight shake.

Little jingle bells can be connected by wire and hung from driftwood trees. Small bells from India, China, Switzerland or other countries can be set atop the rocks. These add a decorative touch as well as a nice sound when gently shaken, a symbol of the connection between heaven and earth.

Water wheel. An attractive fountain feature with a distinctive sound, the water wheel is sometimes found in garden and hardware stores. Adjust the water flow to ensure continuous turning of the wheel.

Water wheel in the bucolic agricultural setting of a previous century. © Nova Development.

Miscellaneous accents.

- Miniature or doll house lawn furniture with a cocktail toothpick umbrella unfurled.

- Lighthouse; if hollow, perhaps shine an underwater light up through the lighthouse.

- Cups filled from above and spilling over.

Readers Respond:

Ben Franklin crafts
"I bought almost all my fountain making supplies when I came upon an entire waterfall department at the Ben Franklin crafts store. I was watching a show 'Everyday Elegance' on AMC Romance Classics Preview, and the host had gone to Chinatown to get dinner party supplies. As the camera followed him through the shops, I noticed many 'fountain bowl' possibilities on the shelves. I thought 'Wow, I might be able to have quite the affordable selection if I go there!' – Marie Brayman, Everett, WA

5 year old nephew
"My fountain turned out to be beautiful! I also helped my five year old nephew make a fountain with shells he has collected."
– Rebecca Walsh, Cincinnati, OH

Mermaid from Copenhagen
A fountain explorer writes, "Your guide began my 'liquids flowing' to make my own table top fountain. Here is a photo of my first fountain

1" tall watering can, flower pot borrowed from the family dolls.

Little Mermaid of Copenhagen, photo © Mrs. Denise Fasano.

that I'm proud of. Guests comment on how soothing it sounds, and they love the design I created. They thought it was store bought!

During our many travels I've collected stones, rocks and items to remind my husband and me of the places we've been. I created this fountain in a tribute to those laces. The wonderful added touch was the 'Little Mermaid sitting on a rock' we purchased when in Copenhagen. I surrounded her with the blue glass stones to represent blue ocean water. The water flows from behind the Little Mermaid down through the blue stones."

– Mrs. Denise A. Fasano, San Diego, CA

An umbrella protects against probable miniature showers in this oval fountain. Photo © Paris Mannion.

Bowl with straw handle contains a recessed fountain; with slate fountainhead, shells, ivy. Student composition, San Francisco Learning Annex, Spring '98. Photo © Paris Mannion.

Etruscan figurine stands on ledge beneath gushing spring (hole drilled in rock); votive candle holder set in back; flower, underwater light. Photo by Greg Hebert.

Water dances off slate and is welcomed by the pool below, as we peek into a fern-lined swimming hole in miniature.

Chapter 7: Tips from the Experts

Drilling

Often the addition of a hole can turn an object into an interesting fountainhead. Perhaps you'd like to place a slate rock chunk over the pump spout. Or maybe you need a hole in a clay saucer or pot, as in the Amphora tutorial later in this chapter. Maybe you want to surprise your son by turning his basketball shoe into a fountainhead, and a hole in the sole will do the trick!

Hole drilled in slate, forming a fountainhead.

Finding a drill press

If you're going to do much drilling, a drill press is invaluable. They are usually more powerful than hand drills, and let you concentrate on making accurate holes. You are less likely to be taken for a ride by a heavy tool with a sharp, spinning bit on the end.

If you don't want to buy one, check the Yellow Pages for masonry and granite companies; they are sure to have drill presses and may work with you on drilling stones. Appreciation in the form of money or food can work miracles.

Benchtop drill presses can be purchased from stores carrying power tools, such as Sears, Harbor Freight Tools, or Post Tool. These have the advantage of taking up less space than floor models and are less costly. However, they can also be less powerful than the full sized models. If possible, test the press – or one with the same horsepower – on a sample of the material you're going to drill.

We've had success drilling slate, dry sandstone, and clay pots with our 1 HP floor model. Wet sandstone can be difficult, but becomes easier to drill if dried in the oven.

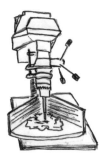

Benchtop drill press with L-shaped drilling jig.

Be safe!

When drilling, follow sensible safety precautions: always wear eye protection (goggles or a face shield) and a dust mask. Tie back loose hair, remove jewelry, and don't wear things which can get caught in the bit - such as long sleeves. Read the owner's manual, have good lighting, and don't work when you're tired.

Be aware that the edges of rock can be sharp and can give you a nasty cut if the workpiece is grabbed and spun by the drill press. If possible, clamp the rock down before drilling to avoid incidents like this. Use strong 2" to 4" clamps; angle paint stirrers or other flat wood pieces across the rock and clamp them in place for greater stability. Or wedge and clamp the rock in the corner of an L-shaped piece of wood, and clamp the whole assembly to your drill press table. When in doubt, turn off the drill press and take a break.

Down to Drilling

Drill your stones at low speed using a sharp carbide tipped masonry bit, 5/8" in diameter (to fit over 1/2" plastic tubing) or 3/8" diameter (to fit over the pump's spout directly). Allow the bit to do the work for you, rather than forcing it down into the stone. You may need to pause every so often to vacuum out the hole or spray water in it to settle the dust and cool the area. Take your time!

There are other approaches to drilling 5/8" holes in rocks for fountainheads. Some borrow a technique from lapidary work which uses oil and lightweight diamond drills to make small holes in small stones. They use a little cooking oil to lubricate the drill and reduce dust. But the oil is not circulating so the bit will get hot quicker than with water. Pouring a little oil into the initial drill impression won't hurt non-porous stone like slate but may absorb into sandstone or lava. The result will be an oil sheen on the fountain water. In the long run, water, not oil, is the best lubricant for drilling large numbers of fountain stones.

Diamond core drill bits are an alternative to the carbide tipped masonry bits. Craft quality diamond bits can be found in some hardware stores and in Harbor Freight and other hardware catalogs. Diamond bits heat up quickly and need water to stay cool. Keep the stone to be drilled wet using a in a spray bottle, turkey baster or IV drip. Or use a small clay ring or donut on top of the stone to act as a reservoir for water.

An expert and modern-day alchemist hard at work in the laboratory.

To minimize fears about working with water and electricity, use a ground fault interrupter (GFI). A GFI, available in hardware stores, will shut off the electric current in milliseconds if it senses a short to ground. The expense of a GFI is small considering the protection it gives against electric shock.

Or use a pneumatic drill. A drill with compressed air will give less torque and may be too high speed for best drilling results. Also the bit will need more water to stay cool due to the higher speed. The exhaust from a pneumatic drill really blows, so use enough water to keep the dust down.

A final suggestion is using a treadle switch or foot pedal as an on/off switch for the drill. A foot treadle is an added safety feature for large production drilling. In case the drill is bound into rock and about to shatter or spin, it is easier to take your foot off the pedal than reach up for the drill's off-on switch. Tool places carry treadle switches; wire it up to the drill or plug the drill into the treadle and the treadle into an extension cord.

Again, my thanks to the fountain makers at ttfountains@onelist.com for their approaches.

After your stones are drilled, build your fountain, plug in the pump and watch water shimmer over the rock as it tumbles down.

The start of building a fountain basket with pump in cup in foreground. Photo © Paris Mannion.

Underwater electric light

This waterproof dazzler dramatically increases the visual effect as the water and light dance before you. Crystals and shells are illuminated from below with clear, red, yellow, blue or green lenses. The Rena underwater light's glass bulb needs to be protected from slipping rocks. Another model of the underwater light is egg shaped; both make great night lights.

Containers

Fountain in a basket

Select a basket woven of straw or other material and fit inside the basket a waterproof bowl at least 2" deep. Build your fountain in the bowl and place it in the basket. Using Spanish moss, silk or dried fronds, birds, air plants, candles, stones, and other accents, fill in the extra area in the basket to create an unusual woodland or beach scene.

By osmosis, water will easily travel from the fountain rocks to surrounding moss. Use care and ingenuity to keep the moss and basket dry.

Painting and Sealing

Perhaps you have bowl whose shape and size you like but prefer a different color. Spray paint with the color you want and finish with four or more coats of waterproof sealant. Spray paint chips off glass and ceramic containers after exposure to circulating water if not fixed with a sealant.

Sand Bowl

Coat the container with resin, shellac or laminating fixative; then, while still wet, submerge the container in fine or playground sand. Let it stay there 24 hours. Two treatments or coats are usually sufficient to cover thin spots and create a natural-looking sand bowl. When completely dry and hardened, dislodge loose sand and seal with at least four coats of waterproof sealant.

Fiberglass pool within a garden

Use fiberglass cloth and epoxy resin to create a watertight container with natural, organic contours. It's perfect to use in a dish garden of living plants, giving the effect of an outdoor scene.

Fiberglass and epoxy resin can be obtained from hardware and marine supply stores. The epoxy comes in a pair of cans, one of resin and one of hardener. It can be pricey, so you may want to share with a friend or build several little pools.

You'll also need the container you're going to build your scene in, a plastic bag, an old nasty paintbrush, and sand. If a beach isn't handy, sandblasting sand from a hardware or garden center works just fine.

Ferns and contrasting foliage textures are a wonderful addition to the fiberglass garden.

Block drainage hole in your planting container and fill it with sand moistened to "sand castle" consistency. Scoop out a pool area in the sand. It should be at least deep enough to cover your pump with water plus about half an inch extra for a safety margin. If the sand isn't holding shape, moisten it with a spray bottle of water.

Once your pool is roughed out, line it with a plastic bag. The plastic will help keep epoxy from soaking through the fiberglass and into the sand. Test the bag beforehand to be sure that it doesn't melt when exposed to the epoxy resin or hardener, or let off noxious fumes.

Fiberglass pool within a dish garden of living plants.

Miniature camera and soda can in fiberglass garden.

Take the fiberglass cloth and lay it on top of the bag, pressing in and around the contours so that it takes on the shape of your pool. When you're happy, do one last test fit with your pump, making sure there's still room for it to sit underwater.

Mix a small batch of the epoxy and resin, following the directions on the can. You may have to guess a bit in order to mix up smaller quantities than the can calls for. Paint the resulting mixture onto the fiberglass cloth, getting into all of the nooks and crannies of your pool. Let it dry.

Repeat the painting process a few times, drying the pool each time. When you can lift it out of the sand/plastic bag and it retains its shape, flip it over, brush off excess sand, and apply epoxy to the outside.

1" tall ceramic philosophers.

When the pool feels fairly sturdy, give it a leak test: fill it with water. If there are leaks, allow it to dry, then apply more epoxy and test it again.

If you wish, you can give your pool a more natural appearance by sprinkling sand or pebbles into a final coat of wet epoxy. Be sure to brush off excess sand when the epoxy is dry, or it may clog your pump.

Once your pool is completed, you can install it in your planting container. The edge of the pool can be disguised with overhanging plants, tamped down soil or sand, pebbles, or rocks.

Handy Supplies

Variation on the mask theme, Place Igor Stravinsky, Paris.

Modeling clay

Pliant modeling clay can be used in chunks to prop up shells or decorative pieces that you have difficulty balancing in the fountain. Polymer clay such as Premo is durable yet easy to work with and comes in beautiful colors that can be blended. Fimo, another polymer clay, is strong and durable but hard to soften to a workable consistency. Sculpey brand modeling clay also works but tends to break apart over time. Polymer clay is a good design stabilizer and often a great solution to the problem of shells or stones slipping or shifting away from where you put them. It is especially effective in creating a two or three tier arrangement of shells overflowing water to the shell below. Modeling clay can be found at art supply and craft stores.

You might make polymer clay figurines to decorate your fountain. As these would be more permanent objects than chunks broken off to stabilize a design, the figurines should be varnished or watersealed for longer life.

A well loved tube of E600, an underwater adhesive.

Epoxy putty

This white or yellow material with a blue center (in hardware stores) can be used to fill in drainage holes in ceramic or water sealed clay bowls that you wish to use as fountain containers. Simply break off a piece about 1/2" long, mash the blue (epoxy) and white (putty) material together, and fit over the hole, smoothing the edges so it blends with the surrounding clay or ceramic. When dry, in about an hour, epoxy putty forms a watertight seal.

E6000 and Goop

These adhesives hold under water and can be used to glue rocks together, if you want to fix your fountain composition permanently. E6000 is found in craft stores; Goop, for shoes, is a glue sealant to be used sparingly. Be sure you can lift the arrangement out to get at the pump when it needs cleaning.

Making a Slumped Glass Fountainhead

A stained glass piece 4-6" in diameter is placed over a mold and heated in a kiln. The glass slumps or melts over the mold. When cool, the piece is inverted and a hole is cut in the center with a glass cutting drill, so that the fountainhead can be placed over the pump spout or tubing. Stained glass stores may offer classes on glass fusing and slumping to make unique bowls and fountainheads.

Step 1:
Score and break a piece of glass about 4" square.

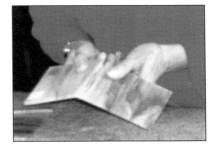

Step 2:
Metal cone mold with leftover white wash on it (prevents glass from sticking to the mold). New wash is added and dried before each firing.

Photos © Paris Mannion

Step 3:
Place the square, oval or circle of glass on the mold; placing it off-center, as we have done, will result in the fountainhead having an irregular shape.

Step 4:
During firing the glass melts or slumps over the cone.

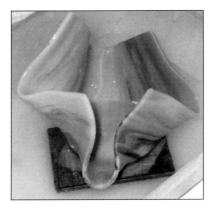

Step 5:
We prepare to drill by placing the slumped glass under water, on a piece of wood.

Step 6:

Manu, a glass drilling expert, shows us how it is done with a specialized 1/2" drill bit. Start drilling just a few degrees short of vertical to let the drill bit get a grip on the glass.

Notice his use of a cordless drill, to avoid the risk of using a tool which is plugged in near water. Managing a cordless drill like this takes some shoulder strength.

Step 7:

The glass fountainhead fits over the pump spout. To elevate the fountainhead, put 1/2" tubing over the pump spout and then step the tubing down with smaller diameter tubing (3/8") which will fit through the glass fountainhead hole.

At right, the fountainhead in use.

Sculptors:
Is there a water fountain bather in you?

A reptile attempting to snack on a distracted bird is restrained by a mermaid at the Piazza Navona, Rome.

Scandalous bather at the Piazza della Reppublica, Rome.

The figures here are made of marble and bronze. Just about any sculptural medium would work to create a charming scene of female bathers splashing in water.

I haven't actually made a water fountain bather. But these Italian Renaissance designs were too good to overlook as potential table top fountains. At left, we see the serpent's upturned head could easily be fitted with a water pipe jetting streams of water on the playful lass. She and other 19th century mermaids in the northern fountain of Rome's Piazza Navona have a centaur's tail as well.

A sister fountain bather luxuriates under a stream of water at the Piazza della Reppublica in Rome. The Fountain of the Naiads, four naked bronze nymphs, caused something of a scandal when it was unveiled in 1901. To the side of a table top fountain bowl, a fish with a pipe in its mouth could be angled to send water onto a reclining figure.

Sculptors, you are the experts here!

Photos © Tanya Inman

Making the Amphora Fountain

An amphora is a tall clay jar with narrow neck and base and two handles hear the neck. Each amphora holds 7 to 8 gallons. The plural of amphora is amphorae or amphoras. Amphorae were used by ancient Greeks and Romans to hold wine, water, oil and honey.

Like the waterfall fountain, the amphora fountain will also be loud when the pump is on full throttle. The amphorae fountain is good for living rooms, foyers, and other larger spaces. With its cups overflowing, the amphorae produce a lovely tinkling sound.

Figure 26
Fountain of the Amphorae,
Rome.

The amphorae fountain in Rome (Fig. 26) can be miniaturized with this table top model which uses four clay pots joined at angles (Fig 27). The top pot has a hole drilled with a 1/2" concrete and masonry bit. A length of 1/2" flexible plastic tubing is threaded through the hole and attached at the bottom to a short 5/8" piece of tubing which fits over the pump spout. Water is pumped up into the top pot where if overflows into the three lower pots and then into the fountain container.

In this design we used clay cups or jars as the fountain centerpiece. The jars, somewhat amphora-shaped, have necks narrower than the body and two handles. Cups and jars, like amphorae, are often symbols of overflowing abundance. They are protective and preserving containers.

Figure 27
Clay pots from Sunnyvale
nursery, Sunnyvale, CA.

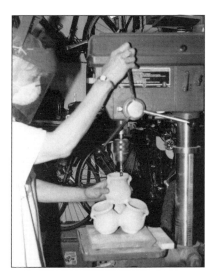

Step 1
Since we'd never drilled terra cotta before, we started by making several test holes in an old clay pot. To our relief, the material drilled very easily.

Drilling was done with a 1/2" masonry bit. To avoid shattering the pot, we applied very little pressure with the drill press, instead letting the drill bit do most of the work. Every few minutes we stopped to vacuum excess dust out of the pot before continuing.

Step 2:
Drilling the cup off center makes it somewhat easier to insert the tubing and to disguise it in the finished fountain.

The finished amphorae fountain set with sandstone and aqua cove rocks, pebbles, and ivy sprigs. Regulate the sound by adjusting the water regulator on the pump.

Making a Horizontal Bamboo Fountainhead

Supplies
Bamboo stakes for making bamboo fountainheads can sometimes be found at Japanese garden nurseries. The 3' - 5' tall stakes, about 1.5" in diameter, sell for around $1.

Step 1:
Cut the bamboo into three 10" to 12" lengths. This design uses three bamboo pieces: two rest on top of the bowl's edge, and the third, with the water lip, crosses the two at right angles.

To make the water pipe, select a bamboo piece with a closed joint near the end. If desired for style, cut a diagonal on this end by the joint so the underside angles in. Make a second diagonal cut at the lip end from which the water will flow. If your piece doesn't have a joint, use epoxy putty to plug up the back so water won't flow out both ends (unless this is what you want).

Wrap the three pieces together with masking tape as shown to stabilize the bamboo for drilling. Using a 1/2" drill bit for boring holes in wood (NOT a carbide drill bit), drill a hole on the underside of the diagonal piece about 3" from the diagonal lip.

Step 2:

If your bamboo fountain will be in constant use, water seal the 3 pieces using a marine sealant such as Pettit's Old Salem Clear Sealer #2018. Follow manufacturers instructions for use. Let dry 24 hours. Or soak the bamboo pipe in Thompson's Water Seal for 24 hours and drip dry on a wire hook like a straightened out coat hanger.

Step 3:

Place 2 pieces parallel to each other and about 2" apart. Center the third piece (with the lip and hole) on top of the two parallel pieces so the hole underneath will be accessible to the pump spout.

Using Superglue or other quick adhesive, glue the three pieces in place to hold the design steady.

Step 4:

When dry and stable in about 20 minutes, wrap the junctures with mildew and water resistant nylon cord or marine cord. Tie with a square knot.

Step 5:
After knotting each cord on the underside, cut the cords about 1/2" from the knot. Using tweezers to hold the base of the cords together, light a match to melt the nylon ends together. This will minimize splitting. Using tweezers will save your fingers.

Step 6:
Place the bamboo fountainhead over your bowl. Does the pump spout reach the hole in the bamboo?

Step 7:
If not, use a small length of 5/8" plastic tubing that fits over the pump spout. Step down the diameter of the tubing by fitting a narrower 3/8" piece of tubing inside the 5/8" piece.

Step 8:
Set the pump's water flow on low or medium and place the pump with bamboo fountainhead in your container. Fill with rocks, greenery and water. Plug it in and enjoy!

Making a Tall Bamboo Fountainhead

Step 1:
Cut two lengths of bamboo. The tall one is hollow all the way through (i.e., no ring in the bamboo); the short one is cut behind a growth ring which seals it so water will only go one way--forward. Cut one end of each piece at an angle; this is a decorative effect for the tall piece and forms the lip for the short one.

Step 2:
Tape the pieces together for easier drilling (see previous bamboo tutorial) and drill a 3/8" hole in near the top and on the side of the tall one. Drill another hole near the growth ring in the short one, also on the side. Water will go up the tall bamboo, out the side hole, into the side hole of the short bamboo, and out the lip of the short bamboo piece.

Step 3:
Fit 3/8" tubing into the side hole of the tall bamboo and also fit tubing into the bottom of this piece. We found a bamboo that took a short length of 3/8" tubing at the bottom. Then we placed another short length of 5/8" tubing over the 3/8" tubing. The 5/8" tubing fits over the pump spout.

Step 4:

Line up the side tubing on the tall piece with the hole of the short piece.

Fit them together. The 3/8" holes may need to be scraped out a little with a knife so the tubing can be wiggled in.

Step 5:

See how your bamboo fountainhead looks from both sides .

Step 6:

Here is the finished bamboo fountainhead in a birdbath container. Adjust the water flow regulator for more or less gushing, depending on the splash factor.

The side piece can be tilted up or down for a variety of water curves.

Birdbath photo © Paris Mannion

132

Water flows from a slumped blue glass fountain head, with dark blue luster gems, rose quartz, tall crystal in background, underwater light. Photo © Paris Mannion, 4/98.

A bamboo spout splashes water into an aqua glass bowl, formerly the home of a citronella candle. Water cascades from the bowl into the larger container and is recirculated; with glossy black rocks, air plant, chunk of blue-green rock. Photo © T.A. Inman

A cat makes her contribution to maintenance by checking the freshness of the fountain's water. Although cats don't care for baths, they do take an active interest in flowing water.

Chapter 8:
Maintaining Your Fountain

The fountain is your living creation so don't hesitate to take it apart and arrange it differently or to clean the pump.

Check water level daily the first week to measure the rate of evaporation; refill with water as needed.

Follow manufacturer's instructions on cleaning the pump. Recommendations vary from once a month with the Cal-Pump sponge filter and screened intake valve, to every 2 or 3 months for fountains with a screened intake valve but no sponge filter. A quick cleaning job involves suctioning the water out of the fountain basin with a meat baster and refilling the basin with clean water. When the cord gets slimy or the water discolored with visible sediment, however, it is time to clean the materials and re-assemble, perhaps with different accents and arrangements.

Unplug the pump and take the whole fountain to a sink. Remove air plants and unattached organic pieces and place in a dry area. Unload the stones and accent pieces. Dislodge the strong little suction cups holding the pump in place and lift it out for cleaning.

A vinegar soak, cream of tartar, or Lime-A-Way can clean off hard water deposits on the bowl, rocks or glass beads. Soak the container and pieces in a mixture of vinegar and water to clean and remove any mineral buildup. A few tablespoons of cream of tartar, in the baking section of grocery stores, dissolved in water will also clean off hard wa-

Use a meat baster to suction out water for a quick cleaning; refill fountain with fresh water.

A man looks over his wellspring as it flows from one level to another, pooling below. Image © Nova Development.

ter deposits. Lime-A-Way can be used also, but not on seashells as they are made of lime. If you are unsure of the material, test a small piece of it first. Another product for dissolving hard water deposits is CLEAR. When you are done, rinse all treasures and pieces thoroughly.

To thoroughly clean the pump, slide or pop off the front cover. This exposes the propeller. Pull out the propeller carefully so as not to bend the blades or break the shaft. Hair, dust and other debris may have collected around the shaft or propeller, slowing the flow of water. Rinse out the pump and reassemble it. Position the pump in the clean container by pressing down so the suction cups once again attach to the bottom.

Some rely on the chlorine in tap water to ensure no algae growth. Others add a mild bleach solution to the fountain water. Add 2 to 3 drops of bleach to a gallon of water, or 1 drop of bleach to half a gallon if your fountain is small. If you can smell a trace of residual bleach or chlorine after 15 minutes, you are done. If there is no smell, add 1 to 2 drops more. You can do this on a weekly basis.

Although most indoor fountains will not develop algae, a product called *fountec* will prevent algae from growing. It was developed for outdoor fountains, and is available at hobby and craft stores and some garden and pottery stores. Read product instruction carefully; *fountec* is toxic to fish and animals (some cats like to drink flowing fountain water).

A product called Fountain Block helps control algae growth in outdoor ornamental water fountains. A small piece of it will help clear cloudy water and remove algae from your indoor fountain. Fountain Block also prevents black discoloration on non-sealed bamboo pipes. The Laguna brand Algae Control for outdoor ponds reduces algae naturally and is "beneficial to aquatic life"; again, read all product instructions carefully.

Caring for your plants: If you root plant cuttings in the fountain water, check the cuttings for debris about once a week.

Air plants such as Tillandsias are members of the Bromeliad family and grow in trees in Mexico and South America. Over 400 species of the plant have been identified to date and are prized by collectors. Tillandsia's lovely flowers and leaf formation make it an attractive fountain accent. Since air plants obtain all nourishment through tiny scales on the leaves, no soil is required. Generally air plants having a smooth green leaves need more water and more light. Mist foliage several times a week with water. Filtered or bottled water is best if water n your area contains salt or minerals. Avoid misting the roots or putting them in water.

Ivy cuttings, a symbol of immortality, friendship and fidelity, grow well in a fountain.

Fertilize by mixing water soluble fertilizer in your spray bottle. Dilute to 1/4 recommended dilution rate. Indirect lighting or shade is best.

Shown in this fountain garden are fern-like air plants that need no soil. Moss and lichen are also founain plants. Student composition, San Francisco Learning Annex, 1998. Photo © Paris Mannion.

A parched pachyderm sips delicately from burbling waters. Elephants may be associated with power, wisdom, peace, happiness, and long life.

Appendix A: Dictionary of Symbols

ANGEL. The angel is a symbol of invisible forces, of the powers ascending and descending between the Source of Life and the world of phenomenon. From the earliest days of culture, angels figure in artistic media, expressing powerful protection and divinity or weakness and evil.

ANIMALS. Animals are frequent images of divine and cosmic forces, as well as the powers of the unconscious and of our instinctive nature, connecting us to our surroundings. Animals in rock paintings may be associated with mythic and religious ideas and ceremonies. Animal-human hybrids can signify the two-fold, corporeal-spiritual nature of humans.

BELL. By its shape the bell is related to the vault of heaven; because of its hanging, suspended position, the bell symbolizes the connection between heaven and earth. The bell calls people to prayer, calls to mind obedience to divine laws, and carries the soul beyond the limits of the mundane. Ringing of the bell in China symbolizes the cosmic harmonies and creative powers. In Islam and Christianity, the sound of bells is likened to the echo of divine omnipotence (the voice of God).

BIRD. Winged beings represent the soul, air, a creative deity, spirits, angels, or supernatural aid, depending on the context. Birds pertain to "heights" and "loftiness" of spirit. In Hindu tradition birds symbolize higher states of being. In ancient Egypt the bird or soul has a human dead. In fairy tales birds may stand for a lover or bear messages. Birds are also symbolic of storms, of forces that are teeming and restless. Like **ANGELS**, birds are symbols of thought, flights of fancy, imagination, and of the swiftness of spiritual processes and relationships.

In the pack of tarot cards designed by Oswald Wirth angels appear frequently to illustrate a variety of different situations and contexts.

Birds: The soul of the deceased departing the body in the form of a bird with human head. After an Egyptian funereal papyrus.

Candle on brass footed stand.

CANDLE. Like the lamp, the lighted candle is a symbol of individuated light, of the life of an individual as opposed to the cosmic and universal light. The candle also symbolizes the relationship between spirit and matter (the flame consumes wax). In fairy tales, death has power over burning candles which represent human lives. In Christianity, candles are symbols of faith and light during Mass, funerals, and processions.

COLORS. Color symbolism is practically universal, for colors affect our moods and feelings. Primary and bright colors have a cheering effect, while dark colors have a more somber effect. Aside from this general distinction, color symbolism is culturally determined. Here we explore color symbolism in China and European-based cultures, but not American Indian cultures.

In the East, focus is on the colors of nature that provide a calming yet invigorating stimulus to body and mind. "The reds, blues, green, yellows and whites of trees, flowers and earth help to inspire and regenerate our ch'i," say Sarah Rossback and Lin Yun in their book *Living Color.* The use of color is one of the nine basic cures of feng shui. The Ba-gua five element color wheel is fundamental to using color in feng shui. The octagon is a map of eight life fortunes with corresponding colors, body parts and directions; the ninth direction is the center.

In the West, a superficial classification suggested by optics relates warm, advancing colors (red, orange, yellow and white) to assimilation, activity and intensity. Cold, retreating colors (blue, indigo, violet and black) correspond to dissimilation, passivity and debilitation, according to H. Cirlot's *Dictionary of Symbols.* Let us look at the interpretations of various colors, keeping in mind that each color has a positive and negative aspect.

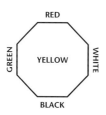

The Ba-gua five element color wheel is fundamental to using color in feng shui.

Red: In China, red is considered a particularly auspicious color for it connotes happiness, warmth or fire, strength and fame. A powerful color, red is an energy source, a stimulator and a way of expelling bad ch'i. In the Ba-gua, red

140

is associated with the fame or rank area.

In the West, red is the color of fire and blood and is symbolically ambivalent. On the one hand, red is the color of passion, fertility, sentiment, love, warmth and the life-giving principle. On the other hand, red is the color of anger, war and fire's destructive power. In alchemy, red is the color of the Philosopher's Stone (the goal of the alchemists) and carries the light of the sun.

Orange. In China, orange, a mixture of red and yellow, is auspicious and is imbued with the characteristics of these colors-happiness and power.

Orange Poppy: a symbol of earth, sleep, and forgetfulness. Image © Nova Development.

In the West, orange is often associated with pride, ambition or even ferocity, cruelty, desperation and egoism, giving it an ominous and tragic character.

Yellow. In China, yellow or gold stands for power; it connotes tolerance, patience and wisdom gained from past experiences. The emperor wore gold robes with a golden dragon. Yellow is contrasted to black and is also its complement; yellow (yang) arises out of black (yin) as the earth arises out of the primal waters. Yellow designates the center of the universe.

In the West, yellow indicates generosity, eternity, transfiguration, intuition and intellect and is an attribute of Apollo, the sun-god. Yellow is associated with the light of the sun, illumination, and dissemination. As the color of autumn, yellow represents ripeness and maturity. It also has a negative interpretation. In the Middle Ages yellow was the color of envy or disgrace; in Islam pale yellow is associated with deception.

Green. In China, green represents tranquillity, hope and freshness and is the color of the wood elements, symbolizing spring growth.

Leaf Mask.

The green of emeralds and lotus leaves indicate good, healthy earth ch'i. Green is associated with the family area on the Ba-gua.

In the West, green is the color of earthly, tangible, growing things; it is the color of Venus and represents the function of sensation. Green is also linked with envy and with decay, decomposition and death.

Blue. In China, blue is a color associated with wood and can symbolize spring, new growth, hope and protection against the evil eye. Blue in the Ba-gua is associated with knowledge and self-cultivation. Blue-green or aqua is more auspicious than true blue as it is nearer to the colors of spring and nature and represents verdant youth (sky blue or young bamboo shoots). On the other hand, blue is a cold secondary color of mourning and often blue is avoided in building projects.

In the West, blue is the color of heaven, distance and water; it is experienced as pure, immaterial and cool. It is the color of truth and fidelity. Blue is the color of Juno and Jupiter and stands for religious feeling, devotion and innocence. Egyptian gods and kings were often depicted with blue beards and wigs. On the other hand, blue can mean sad or morose.

Purple. In China, purple, deep red, or plum is an auspicious color and inspires respect. An individual with "purple ch'i" has a high nobility and is a powerful, rich and fortunate person. Purple in the Ba-gua is associated with the wealth area.

Violet: a symbol of Mary and humility. Image © Nova Development.

In the West, violet represents nostalgia and memories because it is composed of blue (devotion) and red (passion). Purple represents power, spirituality and sublimation. Derived from a shellfish yielding purple dye, genuine purple was reserved for the clothing of kings and priests due to its costliness. Hence it symbolizes power, honor, luxury and prosperity.

142

Brown. In China, brown symbolizes the depth and roots of wood. It gives a heavy feeling and an impression of the passage of time, of autumn, and of leaves turning brown. Tan, on the other hand, represents a new and successful beginning; out of seeming hopelessness, a new possibility arises.

In the West, too, brown is the color of earth and of autumn. In the Middle Ages it was a color of mourning; since the late Middle Ages brown has also had erotic significance.

An autumn leaf turns brown, marking the passage of time. © Nova Development.

Black. In China, black or any dark color gives a feeling of depth in mood and perspective. Black also indicates a lack of hope and may make one feel dark, low and depressed. Black is the color of the feminine principle (yin) and contrasts with its opposite yellow (or sometimes also red) rather than with white, as in the West. In the Ba-gua, black is associated with the career area.

In the West, black is similar to white in that both correspond to the absolute and both can express the abundance of life as well as its total emptiness. Undifferentiated black appears as primal chaos, death or evil (as in black magic); as the color of mourning, it is associated with pain. As the color of night, black shares in the symbolic associations of mother-fertility-mystery-death. Black is thus the color of fertility, mother goddesses and their priestesses. In alchemy, black is the color of the prime matter and pertains to fermentation, putrefaction and penitence. It represents the initial stage of all processes as well as the unconscious wisdom which stems from the Hidden Source (as in "dark night of the soul"). Black also symbolizes time (in contrast to white which represents timelessness and ecstasy). The conception of black and white as opposed symbols of the positive and the negative is very common. This opposition is related to the number two and the myth of the Gemini.

White bridge, black shadow; winter in China.

Container: The virgin as a container of the divine child. after Venetian Rosario della Gloriosa Vergine Maria, *1524.*

White. In China, white represents winter, a dead or dormant state; Chinese mourners wear white robes and the corpse is covered in a white shroud. Chinese avoid sleeping under a white blanket from concern that sleep may turn into death. On the other hand, white in the Ba-gua white is associated with children and creativity.

In the West, white is the color of light, purity and perfection. Like black it is closely associated with the absolute (the beginning, the end, and the union) and is used at marriages (symbolizing innocence and virginity) and in initiations. Angels are often shown clothed in white to symbolize spirit. White, related to gold, also represents illumination, glory and good. While black represents unknown, unconscious wisdom, white stands for known, conscious wisdom, intuition of the beyond, mystic illumination, and the spiritual center. White is also the color of ghosts and specters, and here symbolizes death.

CONTAINER. The container is a symbol of receiving and holding, thus frequently a symbol of the womb. In the Bible, Mary, who receives the Holy Spirit into herself, is the container. The New Testament compares the believer to a container of Grace. The container is also a symbol of the human body, which is interpreted as the container of the soul. Many peoples consider the pouring of liquid from one container to another as a symbol of the reincarnation of the soul.

CORAL. As an aquatic animal often existing in branched or tree form, coral sometimes shares the symbolism of **TREE** and **WATER**. Its symbolic content also embraces the vegetable, mineral and animal realms since it looks like a **PLANT** and has a hard calcified skeleton inhabited by living tissue, an aquatic tree. Its red color relates it to blood.

Coral: The coral tree in the ocean. Image © Nova Development.

DRUMS. Most sacred of all ritual instruments, the drum dates from the Neolithic period. As a feminine and earth bound symbol, drums have religious and spiritual applications the world over.

Eggs, a widely recognized fertility symbol. Photo © Nova Development.

EGGS. As the germ of life, the egg is a widely recognized fertility symbol in ancient spring celebrations. The world egg is central to the creation myths of many cultures, including the Druid and Indian. As the symbol of the totality of all creative forces, the egg was present at the primal beginning, often floating upon the primal ocean. It gave forth from itself the entire world. Many prehistoric tombs in Russia and Sweden have revealed clay eggs, left as a symbol of immortality. Mythic Chinese heroes were sometimes imagined as breaking forth from eggs. The Egyptian God Ra is displayed resplendent in his egg. In Egyptian hieroglyphs the egg represents potentiality, the seed of generation, and the mystery of life.

ELEPHANT. In Asia and India, the elephant is the ruler's steed and symbol of power, wisdom, peace, happiness, and long life. In India and Tibet, the elephant often appears as the bearer of the entire universe and occurs in architecture as a supporting structure. The elephant was associated with prudence and moderation in the Middle Ages because, according to Aristotle, the male elephant remained chaste during the two year pregnancy of its mate.

FAIRIES. Fairies probably symbolize the supernormal powers of the soul; they fulfill humble tasks yet possess extraordinary powers and are prone to sudden and complete transformations. They bestow gifts on the newly born; they can cause people, palaces, and wonderful things to appear out of thin air; and they dispense riches. Their powers are not simply magical but are also the sudden revelation of latent possibilities. Fairies are personifications of the stages in the spiritual life or "soul" of landscapes. In ancient Mesopotamia, for instance, fairies took the form of the Lady of the Plains, the Lady of the Fountain, and the Lady of the Water.

Elephant: The Indian god Ganesha depicted as an elephant. Sculpture from 12th century.

Feather. Image ©
Nova Development.

FEATHER. Feathers correspond to faith and contemplation and to the element of air; for many peoples they are a symbol of vegetation, probably because of their leaf-like appearance. Whether singly or in groups, the feather symbolizes the wind and the creator gods of the Egyptian pantheon (Ptah, Hathor, Osiris). In Egyptian hieroglyphics, the feather enters into the composition of such words as dryness, lightness, emptiness and height. Feather headdress of the American Indian chief is a power symbol closely relating him to the sun and to the demiurgic **BIRD** that shaped the material world. The feather plume on the medieval knight's helmet serves as an attribute of social position.

FIRE. Fire is considered by many peoples to be sacred, purifying and renewing. Its power to destroy is often interpreted as the means to rebirth at a higher level. Fire is associated with strength and spiritual energy as well as animal passion. Fire, like water, is a symbol of transformation and regeneration. In alchemy the value of gold lay in its being a receptacle for **FIRE**, for the essence of gold is fire. It embraces both good (vital heat) and bad (destructive conflagration). Fire is also associated with hell and divine wrath. In the Bible, God or the divine is sometimes symbolized by fire.

Fire: The eye of
Horus holding a
torch. Detail of a
mural in an
Egyptian grave.
Image © Corel
Corporation.

In contrast to **WATER**, often said to arise from earth, fire is often thought to come from heaven or the sun. In China, India and Greece, several fire gods were known. In India, the marriage of fire and water symbolizes their efficacy or power to produce intended results. In Greek natural philosophy, fire is either the origin of all being or one of the elements; it is the transmuting agent since all things derive from and return to fire.

FLAME. The points of contact between the flame and light are significant; the flame symbolizes transcendence itself and light the effect of the transcendental upon the environment. The Greeks represented spirit as gusts of incandescent air.

FLOWERS. In its essence and shape, the flower is symbolic of transitory things, of Spring, and of beauty. In China the flower represents the brevity of life and the short-lived nature of pleasure. In its shape, the flower is an archetypal image of the Center and of the soul. The alchemists called a shooting star or meteor a "Celestial Flower", the flower symbolizing the work of the sun.

Iris. The Greek goddess Iris is the embodiment of the rainbow. Image © Nova Development.

Orange or yellow flowers reinforce sun symbolism; red emphasizes the relationship with animal life, blood, and passion. The "Blue flower" symbolizes the impossible, perhaps an allusion to the "Mystic Center" or the Grail; in Chinese mysticism the "Golden Flower" is a parallel to the Grail story.

FOUNTAIN. Associated with **WATER** and with deep secrets, the fountain represents access to hidden springs and sources. In fairy tales descent into the well often symbolizes the path to esoteric knowledge or to the realm of the unconscious. Plunging into the water of the well corresponds symbolically to drinking a particular elixir that grants immortality, youth and beauty (for example, the Fountain of Youth).

In the Bible the well is symbolically connected to cleansings, purification, blessing, and the water of life. In Arab lands wells with square stone enclosures often represent paradise. Water gushing forth is a symbol of the life-force of Man and of all things. The fountain in its circular basin is an image of the soul as the source of inner life, of spiritual energy, and of individuality.

GARDEN. The garden is a symbol of earthly and heavenly paradise and of the cosmic order. In the Bible the Garden is the image of the primal, sin-free condition of humanity. In the garden of the Hesperides in Greek mythology grew the **TREE** with golden apples, usually interpreted as the Tree of Life. As a refuge from the world, the garden is associated with the oasis and the island.

Stag on a rocky hillside by a fountain stream. ©Nova Development.

A secluded garden. Image © Nova Development.

In the West, the walled garden, entered only through a small portal, symbolizes the obstacles and hardships to be overcome before attaining a higher level of spiritual development. The **FOUNTAIN** in a walled garden symbolizes constancy and truth under difficult circumstances. The enclosed garden also symbolizes the intimate areas of the female body. The garden is a place where Nature is subdued, ordered, selected and enclosed. Thus it is a symbol of consciousness (as opposed to the forest, the unconscious, where things grow wild).

JEWELRY, JEWELS, GEMS. Precious ornaments often set with gems symbolize special status, power, esoteric knowledge, and material riches. The jewels themselves signify spiritual truths. Gems hidden in caves refer to the intuitive knowledge harbored in the unconscious. Glistening specks of color contain some of the symbolic sense of precious stones.

Treasures guarded by dragons allude to the difficulties associated with the struggle for wisdom. In folklore tradition of Hindu, Hellenistic and Arabic beliefs, precious stones once fell from the head of snakes or dragons or originated in their saliva. The guarding "monster" and the guarded "treasure" are a synthesis of opposites. Hebrew liturgy makes use of twelve precious stones (representing twelve months of the year and the Zodiac), each with a magic ability. In a negative sense, jewelry represents vanity and the external appearance of earthly things.

Precious gems signify spiritual truths. Image © Nova Development.

MIRROR. Mirror symbolism is linked with water as a reflector and as part of the Narcissus myth. From earliest times the mirror has been thought as ambivalent. It is a surface which reproduces images and in a way contains and absorbs them. The mirror is also related to moon symbolism; it receives images as the moon receives the light of the sun. The mirror is also a sun symbol because of its clarity. A mirror behind a fountain will expand its energy.

PLANTS. As the lowest and most fundamental of the organic world, plants represent the unity of all living things. In mythology are many examples of the partial or complete transformation of plants into humans and animals and vice versa. Osiris, Attis and Adonis, near-Eastern mythic figures, are closely related to plants. The plant's perpetual change, from growth to flowering, maturation and death, and from sowing to harvest makes the pant kingdom as a whole symbolic of cyclical renewal. Plants in fertile abundance are the essence of Mother Earth. An image of life, plants express the manifestation of the cosmos and the birth of forms.

Rock: Sisyphus with a boulder. After a Greek vase painting.

ROCK. The rock is a symbol of solidity and steadfastness. In the Bible the rock represents the strength and fidelity of God who protects. In Chinese landscape painting the rock or cliff appears as firm, permanent or solid (yang), the opposite of the constantly moving waterfall (yin). Thus the rock denotes integrity and cohesion. Stones are frequent images of the Self because they are complete, unchanging and lasting. In Greek mythology, the boulder that Sisyphus constantly rolls up the mountain and which always rolls down again, represents fruitless efforts, a general symbol of human wishes that are never conclusively satisfied. The rock, like the stone, is held in many traditions to be the dwelling place of a god and the source of human life. Many people today look for stones of special beauty-in rock shops, on beaches, in the hills. Some Hindus pass from father to son stones believed to have magical powers.

SHELL. One of eight emblems of good luck in Chinese Buddhism, shells are also a sign for a prosperous journey because of their association with **WATER**, the source of fertility. The shell is sometimes seen as a symbol of the prosperity of one generation rising out of the death of the preceding generation. Shells are also related to the moon and to Woman (for example, the birth of Aphrodite from a shell).

Serpent: The kundalini serpent and the major channels of the nadi system, depicted as a serpent-entwined staff.

Serpent: The uræus serpent with the sun disk, worn on the forehead of Egyptian kings.

SNAKE, SERPENT. The serpent or snake symbolizes energy itself, pure and simple force, with its ambivalence, moral dualism and diverse roles. The snake's sinuous movements without legs, the way it sheds its skin, its threatening tongue, undulating markings and hiss combine to make it a symbol of aggressive worldly powers, positive and negative. Living in deserts, woods and water, snakes are often guardians of the **FOUNTAINS** of life and of immortality, of the hidden treasure and of the underworld. They are also connected with the masculine principle (phallic shape) and the feminine principle; the Greek goddesses Artemis, Hecate, and Persephone carried snakes in one or both hands. In pre-Columbian America the plumed serpent with **FEATHERS** on its head, tail and body symbolized a union of heaven (feathers) and earth (snake).

As a primordial or primitive strata of life, snakes are often depicted as the principle of evil inherent in all worldly things, a force of vicious destruction. The demonic implications of the snake can be mastered, controlled, and used for higher purposes; the chakra system shows the Kundalini snake of cosmic energy and libido coiled at the base of the spine. As the life force, the snake biting its own tail (the uroborus) is sometimes shown circling the Wheel of Life; as the healer and poisoner, the snake is curled around the staff of Æsculapius, the ancient god of healing arts. Here snakes pertain to resurrection and renewal through molting as well as beneficial uses of its poison which originally caused the injury.

Tree: round dance round a tree idol. Clay figurine from Cypress, ca 1000 B.C.

TREE. Having one of the widest range of meanings, tree symbolism has the most extensive geographical distribution. Representing the **PLANT** kingdom, the tree has been viewed as the image of divine essence or as the birthplace or residence of numinous powers. Trees that renew their foliage annually (deciduous trees) are above all symbols of the rebirth of life and victory over death. The tree's form – roots imprisoned in earth (the underworld), a powerful and vertically ascending trunk (the middle world), and a crown striving toward heaven (the upper world) – has symbolized the union of the cosmic realm and terrestrial life. These aspects contributed to the idea of the world tree or the world axis, which links the three worlds by standing in the center of the cosmos. World axis symbolism goes back to pre-Neolithic times. The leaves and branches of such world trees were said to be inhabited by mythic animals, souls of the dead or the unborn (in the form of **BIRDS**), or by the rising and setting sun and moon.

Tree: Adam, Eve, and the serpent under the tree of knowledge. After a picture in the Codex Vigilanus seu Albeldensis.

In China, and India twelve sun birds inhabit the world tree's branches; these birds represent higher levels of spiritual being and development. The **FOUNTAIN** is frequently related to the tree. The tree bearing fruit and offering shade and protection has been understood as a feminine or maternal symbol, although the erect trunk is usually a phallic symbol.

In Islam, the inverted tree represents the tree of happiness or fortune. In India (Bhagavad Gita) and in Hebrew tradition (Zohar), the inverted tree is a symbol of the unfolding of all being out of a primal ground. The roots represent the principle of all manifestation; the branches, the concrete and detailed reality of this principle. In India, a bride is wed with a tree before marriage to strengthen fertility. The tree appears as the mythical ancestor of humans among various peoples in central Asia, Japan, Korea, and Australia. The association of the tree and **FIRE** is also widespread and probably has to do with attributing life force to the tree. In the wood of certain trees fire is supposedly concealed and is drawn out by rubbing.

In the Bible, the tree appears in double form as the tree of life and the tree of knowledge of good and evil. The tree of life represents the original fullness of paradise and symbolizes the hoped-for fulfillment of the end of time. The tree of

Turtle.

A lighthouse above the dark waters. Image © Nova Development.

Yin and Yang: adapted as trademarks for macrobiotic foods.

knowledge, with its seductive fruits, represents the attraction of acting contrary to divine commandments.

In China, three popular trees, symbolizing longevity and fertility, are the bamboo, the cherry tree, and the pine, called the "three friends" because all are evergreen. Psychoanalysis sees in the tree a symbolic reference to the mother, to spiritual and intellectual development, or to death and rebirth.

TURTLE. The Chinese observed that the turtle has a SHELL rounded on top to represent heaven and square underneath to represent earth. The turtle is a symbol of material existence, natural evolution, longevity and slowness.

WATER. Water is a symbol of a complex range of meanings. As an unformed, undifferentiated mass, it symbolizes the abundance of possibilities; water also represents the primal origin of all being, the first matter, and occurs in numerous creation myths. The Chinese consider water as the specific abode of the dragon because all life comes forth from the waters.

In China, water is assigned to the yin (female) principle; in other cultures water is similarly associated with the feminine, the depths, and the moon. Water is identified with intuitive wisdom, natural life, and potentiality, which precede form and creation.

In Islam, Hinduism, Buddhism, and Christianity, water is a symbol of bodily, emotional, and spiritual cleansing and the power of renewal. Immersion in water, as during baptism, intensifies the life-force. Its qualities of transparency and depth are also associated with the transition between fire and air (ethereal) and earth (material). Water is the universal symbol of fertility and life; likewise, spiritual fertility and spiritual life are often represented by water. Water can also have a negative symbolic meaning as a destructive force or flood. Psychoanalysis regards water primarily as a symbol of the feminine and of the powers of the unconscious, a fluid body.

WATERFALL. The waterfall is an important motif in Chinese landscape painting. Its plunging downward is seen as the opposite of the upward striving cliff or **ROCK.** The waterfall (Yin) is considered to represent the opposite of the cliff's immobility (Yang). The waterfall's seemingly constant form, which endures the continual change of the flowing water, is regarded in Buddhism as a symbol of the insubstantiality of everything worldly.

Waterfall, enduring the continual change of flowing water. © Nova Development.

WINDCHIMES. A small set of wind chimes can be placed in the fountain container. Chimes moderate or change chi flow; the sound will help focus your mind as well as relax you.

Two orchid stems in pin frog, crystal cluster, underwater light, and black bowl. Photo (c) Paris Mannion.

A lone droplet contemplates leaving its home in the fluffy-ruffle clam to visit the amethyst crystal below.

Appendix B: Fountain Parts and Accents

Search the Web to find more

Animal figurines, crystals, beads, rose quartz candle holders:

South Pacific Wholesale Co., Vermont
1-800-338-2162
sopacvt@aol.com
http://www.beading.com

Bamboo stakes & pieces:

Yamagami Nursery, California
1-408-252-3347

L& L Nursery Supplies
wholesale in larger quantities
1-510-651-4900.

Bowls:

Create Your Indoor Fountain, California
1-800-828-5967
http://www.buildfountains.com
Gold pans (black) 10.5" to 17" diameter

Fountain Pumps, Inc., California
1-800-207-3479
(wholesale orders with retail seller's license)
Gold pans (black) 10.5" to 17" diameter
Send $2 for catalog

The Plant Stand, California
1-800-698-1077

Water jet used in fountain. Photo © Paris Mannion.

Miniature ceramic fountain bridge from Sunnyvale Nursery.

Finished Fountains:

Fountain Central, Washington
1-253-539-5185
http://www.fountaincentral.com
(a variety of fountain artists show their wares, good prices, quality fountains)

Fountain foggers or misters:

Create Your Indoor Fountain, California
1-800-828-5967
http://www.buildfountains.com

Fountain Pumps, Inc., California
1-800-207-3479
(wholesale orders with retail seller's license)
Send $2 for catalog

Fountain Kits:

Create Your Indoor Fountain, California
1-800-828-5967
http://www.buildfountains.com
(abalone; drilled slate and sandstone fountain-heads)

Fountain Builder, Colorado
http://www.fountainbuilder.com
(hand crafted feather rock fountainhead)

The Fountain Company, California
1-800-955-7868
http://www.egglite.com

Prosperity Fountain, New York
1-800-804-7240
http://www.prosperityfountain.com

Tranquil Furnishings, Oregon
http://www.specialweb.com/tranquil
(agate, jasper and shell fountainheads)

Pumps:

Aquatics Direct Ltd, UK
01260-275144
Fax: 01260-298141
http://www.aquatics-direct.com

Remote control to turn fountain on and off.

Create Your Indoor Fountain, California
1-800-828-5967
http://www.buildfountains.com
Hagen Aquapump 1
Ask about the Rena pump and light combo

Fountain Builder, Colorado
http://www.fountainbuilder.com
United Pump, Inc., pumps, pump & light combo

The Fountain Company, California
1-800-955-7868
http://www.egglite.com

Fountain Pumps, Inc., California
1-800-207-3479
(wholesale orders with retail seller's license)
Send $2 for catalog
Ask about the Rena pump & light combo

Tranquil Furnishings, Oregon
http://www.specialweb.com/tranquil
Rio pumps

WaterHeart, Washington
http://www.waterheart.com/pumps.htm
Rio pumps

Remote Control (turn your fountain off and on from a distance with a garage door remote):

Create Your Indoor Fountain, California
1-800-828-5967
http://www.buildfountains.com

Fountain Pumps, Inc., California
1-800-207-3479
(wholesale orders with retail seller's license)
Send $2 for catalog

Rock:

Fallen Stone
1-801-673-2349

Shells:

U.S. Shell, Texas
1-956-943-1709
http://www.usshell.com
(min. order $150; go in with friends)

Stones, polished :

Craft stones
1-619-789-1620

Nature's Emporium
http://natures-emporium.com/
crystals, fluorite, and gems galore

St. John's Rock
1-520-337-4459

Stones, specimen:

Jewell Tunnel Imports
1-813-814-2257

Nature's Emporium
http://natures-emporium.com/
crystals, fluorite, and gems galore
1-253-826-0510

Village Originals
1-803-760-3050

Underwater glue:

E-6000
Create Your Indoor Fountain, California
1-800-828-5967
http://www.buildfountains.com

E-6000
Fountain Pumps, Inc., California
1-800-207-3479
(wholesale orders with retail seller's license)
Send $2 for catalog

Bell spray used in fountain. Photo © Paris Mannion.

Underwater lights:

Create Your Indoor Fountain, California
1-800-828-5967
http://www.buildfountains.com

The Fountain Company, California
1-800-955-7868
http://www.egglite.com

Fountain Pumps, Inc., California
1-800-207-3479
(wholesale orders with retail seller's license)
Send $2 for catalog

Water jets and bell sprays:

Create Your Indoor Fountain, California
1-800-828-5967
http://www.buildfountains.com

Fountain Pumps, Inc., California
1-800-207-3479
(wholesale orders with retail seller's license)
Send $2 for catalog

Chinese statuette, a happy veteran of many fountain-building classes.

Footnotes

Introduction

1. Webster defines "alchemy" as associated with the Greek "to melt and pour" and is an early form of chemistry. Alchemy is "a method or power of transmutation; esp. the seemingly miraculous change of a thing into something better."

Chapter 1

2. The four rivers are the Ganges, the Plate, the Danube and the Nile.

3. Lao-tsu, *Tao Te Ching,* ed. Stephen Mitchell (Harper Perennial, NY, 1991), verses 8, 15, 76, and 78. Lao-tsu teaches compassion, patience, and simplicity.

4. Kiyoshi Seike, Masanobu Kudo, & David Engel, A Japanese Touch for Your Garden (Tokyo, NY: Kodansha International, 1980, 1987), p. 38. J.Harada, *The Gardens of Japan,* (London: Studio LTD, 1928) p. viii.

5. Judith Chatfield, *A Tour of Italian Gardens* (NY: Rizzoli International Publ., 1988) p. 11.

6. The English word 'paradise' is a transliteration of the old Persian word pairidaeza, referring to a walled garden (Moynahan, 1979, p. 1). "Paradise" meaning garden first appeared in Middle English as Paradis in 1175.

7. *San Jose Mercury News,* Saturday, April 18, 1998.

8. Craig Campbell, *Water in Landscape Architecture* (NY: Van Nostrand, 1978) p. 7.

9. *Fons Sapientiae: Renaissance Garden Fountains,* by Elizabeth B. MacDougall (ed.), 1978, is a rich source for Italian fountains. The Grolier Multimedia Encyclopedia, 1996, compares fountains from around the world.

10. MacDougal, p. 96.

11. Fountain decorations include cornucopias, urns, fish, wine sacks and bowls. Mythological figures include the nine Muses, Diana, Pan, Apollo, Pegasus, various river gods, and Æsculapius, the ancient healer.

Chapter 2

12. Richard Heinberg, "A Sense of Place," *Intuition,* January, February 1996, p. 19.

13. In J.E. Cirlot, *Dictionary of Symbols* (1962), p. 366.

14. Sarah Rossbach and Lin Yun, *Living Color* (1994), 148-149.

15. Terah Kathryn Collins, *The Western Guide to Feng Shui: Creating Balance, Harmony, and Prosperity in Your Environment.* Hay House (Carlsbad, CA: 1996) p. 55.

16. Former Soviet Union researches provide evidence of the positive health effects of exposure to high doses of negative ions. Abstract from *Muscle & Fitness.* Oct. 1993, Vol. 54, No. 10, p. 59-60.

17. Non Bo, Serenity in a Microcosm, The San Diego Union-Tribune, 6/27/99, H-1.

18. Peg Streep, *Altars Made Easy: A Complete Guide to Creating Your Own Sacred Space* (Harper, San Francisco, 1997), p. 77. She describe creating a workplace altar and the symbolism of accents on pp. 31-33. "By creating sacred space where we work, we signify our presence there and our intention to use the time we spend at work as fruitfully as possible."

19. Lynda McCullough "Where Wonders Settle," *Common Boundary* (Nov-Dec, 1997, pp. 38-41), p. 38.

20. Streep, op. cit., p. 83.

Chapter 3

21. Marie Louise von Franz, *Creation Myths* (1979).

22. The Maidu myth relates that the Earth Maker swam on the wa-

ter and anxiously said, "I wonder how and where and I wonder in which place we could find land in this world." von Franz, op. cit., 117.

23. von Franz, op. cit., 27.

24. C.J. Jung, *Memories, Dream, Reflections* (1963), par. 40.

25. Report on California's Gold Rush, *San Jose Mercury News,* spring 1998. "Gold was refined using mercury from the Middle Ages until the late 19th century, when a new, more efficient method that used sodium cyanide to dissolve the gold was introduced."

26. A. Jaffè, *C.F. Jung: Word and Image* (1979), 106.

27. CW, 14, par. 756-757.

28. CW 16, par. 409.

29. C.J. Jung, *Man and His Symbols* (1964), 162.

Fountain basket, water spout in center, is set off with tall airplants, smooth rocks. "Learn the secrets and pleasures of developing your own unique composition of materials to create a personal fountain." Robert Birnbach, photographer; Susan Picklesimer, artist (415-921-7902).

Bibliography

Campbell, Craig. *Water in Landscape Architecture.* NY: Van Nostrand, 1978.

Cave, Philip. *Creating Japanese Gardens.* Charles E. Tuttle Co., Inc.: Boston, Rutland, Vermont, Tokyo, 1993.

Chatfield, Judith. *A Tour of Italian Gardens.* NY: Rizzoli International Publ., 1988.

Cirlot, J. E. *A Dictionary of Symbols.* 2nd ed. NY: Philosophical Library, 1983.

Collins, Terah Kathryn. *The Western Guide to Feng Shui: Creating Balance, Harmony, and Prosperity in Your Environment.* CA: Hay House, 1996.

Farmer, Penelope (ed.). *Beginnings: Creation Myths of the World.* NY: Antheum, 1979.

Giovetti, Paola. *Angels: The Role of Celestial Guardians and Beings of Light.* ME: Samuel Weiser, Inc., 1983

Grolier Multimedia Encyclopedia. Grolier Electronic Publishing, Danbury, CT: 1996.

Hamilton, Edith. *Mythology: Timeless Tales of Gods and Heroes.* NY: Mentor Book, 1942.

Harada, J. *The Gardens of Japan.* London: Studio LTD, 1928.

Heinberg, Richard, "A Sense of Place," *Intuition,* Jan.-Feb., 1996.

The Herder Symbol Dictionary. Translated by Boris Matthews. Wilmette, IL: Chiron Publications, 1990.

Jaffe, Aniela (ed.). *C. G. Jung, Word and Image.* Princeton, NJ: Princeton University Press, 1979.

_____ (recorder and editor). *Memories, Dreams, Reflections: C. G. Jung.* Translated by Richard and Clara Winston. New York: Pantheon Books, 1963.

Jung, C. G. Collected Works. Vol. 13: *Alchemical Studies*. Princeton, NJ: Princeton University Press, 1983.

_____ (ed.). *Man and His Symbols*. New York: Anchor Press, 1954.

_____. C. W. Vol. 12. *Psychology and Alchemy*. Princeton, NJ: Princeton University Press, 1989.

_____. C. W. Vol. 6. *Psychology and the Transference*. Princeton, NJ: Princeton University Press, 1985.

_____. C. W. Vol. 5. *Symbols of Transformation*. Princeton, NJ: Princeton University Press, 1976.

Lao-tsu. *Tao Te Ching,* ed. Stephen Mitchell. NY: Harper Perennial, 1991.

Lidz, Jane (photos) and Charles W. Moore (text). *Water and Architecture*. NY: Harry N. Abrams, Inc., Publishers (pre-publication copy).

MacDougall, Elizabeth B. (ed.). *Fons Sapientiae: Renaissance Garden Fountains*. Washington, D. C.: Dumbarton Oaks, 1978.

McCullough, Lynda , "Where Wonders Settle," *Common Boundary,* Nov.-Dec., 1997, p. 38-41 p. 38

Morton, H. V. *The Fountains of Rome*. NY: The Macmillan Co., 1966.

Moynahan, E. *Paradise as a Garden in Persia and Mughal, India*. NY: George Braziler, 1979.

Nash, Helen and C. Greg Speichert. *Water Gardening in Containers: Small Ponds Indoor and Out*. NY: Sterling Publishing Co., Inc., 1996.

Neumann, Erich. *The Great Mother*. Translated by Ralph Mannheim. Princeton, NJ: Princeton University Press, 1955.

Plumptre, George. *Garden Ornament: Five Hundred years of History and Practice*. Thames and Hudson, 1989.

Rossbach, Sarah. *Interior Design with Feng Shui.* NY: Penguin Books, 1987.

_____ and Lin Yun. *Living Color: Master Lin Yun's Guide to Feng Shui and the Art of Color.* NY: Kodansha International, 1994.

Smith, Sir William. *Smaller Classical Dictionary.* NY: E.P. Dutton, 1958.

Seike, Kiyoshi; Kudo, Masanobu; and Engel, David. *A Japanese Touch for Your Garden.* Tokyo, NY: Kodansha International, 1980, 1987.

Streep, Peg. *Alters Made Easy: A Complete Guide to Creating Your Own Sacred Space.* Harper San Francisco, 1997.

Swindells, Philip. *Container Water Gardens: Simple-to-Make Water Features and Fountains for Indoor and Outdoor Gardens.* Pownal, VT: Storey Books, 1988.

Symmes, Marilyn, ed. *Fountains Splash and Spectacle: Water and Design from the Renaissance to the Present.* NY: Rizzoli International Publications, Inc., 1998.

Venturi, Francesco (photos) and Mario Sanfilippo (text). *Fountains of Rome.* NY: The Vendome Press, 1996.

von Franz, Marie-Louise. *Creation Myths: Patterns of Creativity Mirrored in Creation Myths.* Zurich, Switzerland: Spring Publications, 1972.

Wilson, Eva. *Ancient Egyptian Designs for Artists and Craftspeople.* NY: Dover Publications, 1986.

Wright, James E., Ph.D. "Recuperation: Charged for Recovery," *Muscle and Fitness* (Oct. 1983), 59-60.

Zimmer, Heinrich. *Myths and Symbolism in Indian Art and Civilization.* NY: Harper and Row, 1946.

A faucet fixture fits over the pump's tubing and flows from a small bowl into the larger clay container. Be sure to water seal porous clay bowls or water will seep through. Student composition, Palo Alto Adult Education, 4/98.

Water jumps from smooth cobble stones, framed by an amethyst cluster. Unlike slate, cobble stone is very hard and requires a diamond drill bit.

Index

Your Ideas & Inspirations

Accents:

Containers:

Plants:

Designs:

Setting/Location

Your Ideas & Inspirations

Accents:

Containers:

Plants:

Designs:

Setting/Location

Order Form

Telephone Orders call 1-800-828-5967 with credit card.

On-line orders paris@buildfountains.com with credit card or
print out order form found at
http:/www.buildfountains.com

Postal orders: Indoor Fountains
Paris Mannion
P. O. Box 632864
San Diego, CA 92163
USA

___ copies of *Create Your Indoor Fountain* @ $17.99 each + $3.50 S&H
+ CA tax if applicable

You may return any books for a full refund – for any reason, no
questions asked.

Company name: _____

Name: _____

Address: _____

City: _____ State: _____ Zip: _____

Telephone: (__) _____ email: _____

Payment:
_____ money order
_____ check
_____ credit card

Order Form

Telephone Orders call 1-800-828-5967 with credit card.

On-line orders paris@buildfountains.com with credit card or
print out order form found at
http:/www.buildfountains.com

Postal orders: Indoor Fountains
Paris Mannion
P. O. Box 632864
San Diego, CA 92163
USA

___ copies of *Create Your Indoor Fountain* @ $17.99 each + $3.50 S&H
+ CA tax if applicable

You may return any books for a full refund – for any reason, no
questions asked.

Company name: _____

Name: _____

Address: _____

City: _____ State: _____ Zip: _____

Telephone: (__) _____ email: _____

Payment:
_____ money order
_____ check
_____ credit card